LUCIEN LAGRANGE

THE SEARCH FOR ELEGANCE

LUCIEN LAGRANGE

THE SEARCH FOR ELEGANCE

WRITTEN BY ROBERT SHAROFF   PHOTOGRAPHS BY WILLIAM ZBAREN

images
Publishing

Published in Australia in 2008 by
The Images Publishing Group Pty Ltd
ABN 89 059 734 431
6 Bastow Place, Mulgrave, Victoria 3170, Australia
Tel: +61 3 9561 5544 Fax: +61 3 9561 4860
books@imagespublishing.com
www.imagespublishing.com

Copyright © The Images Publishing Group Pty Ltd 2008
The Images Publishing Group Reference Number: 759

National Library of Australia Cataloguing-in-Publication entry:

Lucien Lagrange : the search for elegance.

Bibliography.

ISBN 9781864702972.

1. Lucien Lagrange Architects. 2. Architectural firms – Illinois – Chicago. 3. Architecture, Modern – 20th century. 4. Architecture, Modern – 21st century. I. Title. (Series : Master architect series).

720.9773

Designed by Liska + Associates, Chicago, USA

Digital production by Splitting Image Colour Studio Pty Ltd, Australia

Printed by Everbest Printing Co. Ltd. in Hong Kong/China

IMAGES has included on its website a page for special notices in relation to this and our other publications. Please visit www.imagespublishing.com.

IN MEMORY OF MY PARENTS

Lucien Lagrange Sr.
(1908–1995)

Flora Briand Lagrange
(1916–2000)

THE SEARCH FOR ELEGANCE

THE SEARCH FOR ELEGANCE

By Robert Sharoff

"He who, without betraying the modern conditions of a programme, or the use of modern materials, produces a work which seems to have always existed…can rest satisfied. Astonishment and excitement are shocks which do not endure; they are but contingent and anecdotic sentiments. The true aim of art is to lead us dialectically from satisfaction to satisfaction, until it surpasses mere admiration to reach delight in its purest form." (Auguste Perret)

The Chicago architectural community has never quite known how to classify Lucien Lagrange. Is he a Modernist? Certainly, his early career as a designer at Skidmore Owings & Merrill, where he worked with such legendary figures as Bruce Graham and the late Fazlur Khan, would seem to imply as much.

His later work, too, betrays a deep understanding of and love for many of the principal tenets of Modernism: the emphasis on logic and problem solving, the importance of form and clearly expressed structure.

But Modernism in Chicago for the last half century has traditionally been associated with the ideas of Mies van der Rohe—and Lagrange is no huge fan of Mies. In fact, he believes the city's architecture community has been warped by its long obsession with Mies' impossibly strict "less is more" credo.

Is he a Post Modernist? No. He rejects that movement as an intellectual and aesthetic dead end. But what are observers to make of Lagrange's subsequent embrace of a broad range of historical styles—everything from Gothic to Second Empire to Art Deco?

Lagrange's final building at Skidmore was One Financial Place, a large, mixed use project in the Loop that—while displaying a rather un-Skidmore-like interest in street level detail and pedestrian amenities—remains firmly in the Modernist canon.

His first project as an independent architect was Plaza Escada, a four-story retail building on Michigan Avenue executed in brick and buff colored stone that includes ornamental columns around the entryway, a richly detailed Second Empire cornice, and a mansard roof.

It remains, by almost any standard, one of the more astonishing transitions in Chicago architecture. For Lagrange, however, it represented both a return to fundamental principles and the first step in moving beyond the outmoded pieties of Modern architecture.

Today, when a revived Modernism is once again a major force in design, it can be difficult to remember just how stultifying "Modern" architecture had become in the late 1970s and 80s. The writer Tom Wolfe got the tone exactly right when he spoke of the "row after Mies van der Rohe" of impersonal glass boxes that constituted the downtowns of most major American cities during this period.

The situation was especially acute in Chicago, home of Mies and the Illinois Institute of Technology, the school most identified with Miesian Modernism.

What had begun in the first half of the 20th century at the Bauhaus and other design laboratories as a sincere attempt to come to grips with new materials and building methods ended as a stifling orthodoxy every bit as rigid and constricting as the era's more extreme political movements. (Anyone who has ever sat through a discussion—at one time fairly common in Chicago architectural circles—about whether an exposed I-beam constitutes ornament will know exactly what I'm talking about.)

The inflexibility of the Modernists was legendary and, in retrospect, a little bizarre. Historically inspired forms or ornament of any kind were grounds for censure. Similarly, attempts to broaden the parameters of Modernism to include more experimental work were discouraged. Design seemed stuck.

Looking back, both the rise of the historic preservation movement in the 1980s and 90s and the simultaneous popular embrace of Post Modernism can be seen as responses to a cultural conversation that had gotten a little too one-sided. Both movements sought validation and fresh inspiration from the past.

So did Lagrange. The apartments and hotel rooms he has designed over the last 20 years are widely considered to be some of the most elegant and comfortable in the city. They also draw freely from the styles of the past.

In a profile I wrote several years ago, I noted that, "Lagrange loves what most modern architects would consider wasted space—niches and galleries and anterooms and vestibules—along with curved walls, coved ceilings and the kind of retro spaces, such as stone-floored 'orangeries,' that recall a much earlier era of gracious living."

Those words are still relevant. Since then, however, he has also staged a triumphant return to Modernism with several ultra-contemporary steel and glass apartment buildings that more or less brings him full circle and completes what has been a remarkable—if quixotic—grand tour of architectural history.

None of this, of course, has gone unnoticed in architectural circles. "Tell Lucien to stay stiff," said Bruce Graham, Lagrange's Skidmore mentor, in the profile noted above. "He needs to pick a direction and not float around."

I would argue, however, that "floating around" is exactly what Lagrange does best and that the city is the richer for it.

Actually, if one sorts through the criticism Lagrange has received, it mainly comes down to the fact that he regards Modernism as a historic style no different from other historic styles—appropriate for some projects but certainly not for all. It is an approach grounded in architectural process and the realities of the real estate market.

The most salient facts about Lagrange as a designer are that his childhood and training as an architect all took place far from the American architecture wars of the mid-20th century, that period when the combined forces of the International Style were consolidating their hold on the architectural establishment.

Lagrange was born and grew up in France, absorbing first the Beaux Arts glories of Paris and, later, after his parents relocated to the south, the medieval relics of Provence. His father was a mason, his mother a housewife.

He is still—even after 30-plus years in Chicago— reflexively French in his outlook, not least in his belief that Paris is the ideal against which all other cities must be measured. Lagrange loves the romance of Paris and also the humanity—the swank of the Ritz but also the charm of old neighborhoods with solid apartments, good cafes, and a tobacconist or two.

At times, he can sound almost baffled that Americans are willing to deny themselves what are, after all, fairly elementary urban pleasures. "Why can't we have this in Chicago?" he will ask about everything from a romantic rooftop garden to a glorious wrought iron grill. Indeed, why not?

In 1957, Lagrange dropped out of high school and, following his older brother, Michel, immigrated to Canada. Eventually, he decided to become an architect and—in 1966—enrolled at McGill University in Montreal.

McGill in the 1960s represented an alternative to both Harvard University and the Illinois Institute of Technology, the two leading American architecture schools of the period. Both of the latter institutions were dominated by leading Bauhaus high priests: Walter Gropius at Harvard and Mies at IIT.

Detail, façade, Kingsbury on the Park

McGill, on the other hand, was largely under the sway of Peter Collins, a ferociously learned British architect and critic who began his career working for the pioneering French Modernist, Auguste Perret.

Collins took the long view. In his signature book, *Changing Ideals in Modern Architecture*, published in 1965, he downplayed the idea of Modernism as a 20th-century development and instead stressed its conceptual roots in 17th-century Enlightenment thinking. The aim was to throw a wrench into the International Style juggernaut and encourage a more multi-faceted approach to architecture and design that left room for historical and traditional cultural references.

Indeed, as long as architects observe the key modern virtues of functionality and honest expression of materials, they "should feel no shame at adopting archaic forms and techniques in order to harmonize new buildings with an existing architectural environment," he wrote.

He also believed that style is largely about market forces and popular taste and is thus endlessly mutable and recyclable.

Put these two theories together and, essentially, you have Lagrange's design philosophy. Whereas the Modernists of the period demanded a clean break with the past, Lagrange was taught to embrace it as a direct source of inspiration.

The other major influence on Lagrange during this period was Norbert Schoenauer, a Hungarian architect and academic who taught housing. In his lectures and writings, Schoenauer barely mentioned aesthetics. His concerns were mainly sociological. As much planner as architect, he stressed the importance of designing housing that fits the needs and lifestyles of different groups and classes. He also believed in the primacy of the floor plan, an approach Lagrange embraces to this day.

After graduating from McGill in 1972, Lagrange worked briefly for a planning firm in Montreal. During his last three years in school, however, he had had summer internships with Skidmore, which brought him into contact with Bruce Graham. A job offer eventually materialized.

Skidmore at that time was at the apex of its reputation as corporate America's favorite architecture firm. In 1969, Graham had designed the John Hancock Center on Michigan Avenue, the distinctive diagonal bracing of which would find its way onto more than one of Lagrange's subsequent buildings. The Sears Tower, at the time the world's tallest building, followed in 1974.

Skidmore, Miesian to the core, was less about style for Lagrange than about learning how to manage and assemble large, complicated projects. Many of the buildings he worked on were mixed-use facilities containing differing combinations of offices, hotel rooms, condominiums and commercial space. Under the direction of Graham, Lagrange designed seven major buildings during his tenure at the firm. Two of the most impressive were Onterie Center and One Financial Place, both in Chicago.

The former, a 59-story reinforced concrete tower with diagonal bracing on the exterior, was the last project completed by Fazlur Khan, the legendary structural engineer responsible for the Sears Tower and the John Hancock Center as well as numerous other structures. Onterie—the name refers to the two streets that border the project, Ontario and Erie—occupies an irregular site and includes both offices and residential condominiums. The organization, which includes separate entrances, lobbies and elevators for the different functions, is impressive. To my eyes, however, the overall lack of detail along with the heavy, rectilinear quality of the design seems more Graham than Lagrange. (It is interesting to compare Onterie with a later Lagrange project, the condominium building Erie on the Park. There—and unlike Onterie—the asymmetrical nature of the site is brilliantly reflected in the design of the tower.)

One Financial, in many ways, is a bigger departure. It's an enormous structure and a complicated one—a 40-story highrise plus a three-story midrise, the latter constructed over an expressway in downtown Chicago. The different components include a trading room for the Midwest Stock Exchange, a small hotel, offices, parking, a health club, a luxury restaurant, and a commuter train station.

Again, the organization is impressive. It is a complex that must accommodate thousands of disparate visitors a day entering and exiting from a multitude of entrances in a way that minimizes chaos and confusion. This it does, largely by routing the train passengers around, rather than through, the larger structure.

Probably the biggest departure, however, is the façade of the midrise, which includes a row of massive, two-story arches executed in polished brown granite. The arches recall the original home of the Exchange, architect Louis Sullivan's now demolished 1894 Chicago Stock Exchange Building on LaSalle Street.

It was the most overt reference to a previous building or era in the firm's history and a clear sign that at least someone at Skidmore was having second thoughts.

One Financial was completed in 1985. The same year, Lagrange—aware of the chaos that was descending on the firm in the wake of Graham's retirement and an ongoing power struggle between Skidmore's two headquarters offices in Chicago and New York—departed and set up his own firm, Lucien Lagrange Architecture. He was the only employee.

The late 1980s and early 90s were a confusing—though at times exhilarating—period architecturally. Whatever the drawbacks of Post Modernism, it did loosen people up. What was offensive about it ultimately was the lack of sincerity along with a complete disregard for any qualities other than those of decoration.

To the degree that it encouraged architects to move beyond the narrow range of what was then considered Modern, however, it opened the door for Lagrange's numerous stylistic experiments over the next two decades

Lagrange's strengths as a designer, it seems to me, are an instinctive civility and humanity, a formidable knowledge of architectural history and lost light and, most importantly, a fundamental respect for architectural process.

The first two of these are evident to anyone who has ever encountered a Lagrange building close up. Park Tower, for example, with its lively interplay of colors, textures, and detailing as well as the superb way it frames one of the most prominent sites in downtown Chicago, succeeds brilliantly at evoking the breezy urbanity one associates with the world's great avenues and boulevards.

Similarly, the renovation Lagrange undertook several years ago of the Insurance Exchange Building in the Loop, a Neo Classical office building originally designed by D.H. Burnham & Co. in 1912, reveals a sensibility attuned to the dance of urban life—the mix of art and commerce that makes the city such a seductive environment.

The building is located in the heart of the city's financial district, an area dominated by similarly sober buildings that—while at times impressive—one would have a hard time describing as welcoming. The Insurance Exchange Building is neither a masterpiece nor a monstrosity. It's a workhorse of a structure—huge, well located, serviceable. The problem – since it was largely empty—was to wake it up, to reintroduce it to a business community that had moved on to other, newer buildings.

Lagrange's solution was a bold infusion of color and light — a more or less complete re-imagining of the building's public spaces with just enough detail visible from the street to pique the interest of passersby who have been walking or driving by the building for years without giving it a second thought.

His love of history and what I think of as lost light are inescapable parts of his method. Lagrange is one of the few contemporary architects — certainly in Chicago — capable of designing everything from 19th-century Parisian "hotel particuliers" to 21st-century steel and glass skyscrapers.

Style has to come from somewhere, of course. In Lagrange's work, more often than not, it comes from context, both literal and metaphorical.

The immediate inspiration for 840 North Lake Shore Drive, a condominium building, is the Blackstone Hotel on Michigan Avenue, a 1908 Beaux Arts gem by the firm of Marshall & Fox with an exquisitely rendered Second Empire roof. The latter building, however, is only a starting point. Lagrange excels with small sites and irregular sites and 840 has both. The result is a stylish amalgam of Classical detailing — that astounding roof! — and Modern proportions that probably shouldn't work but does due to the overall restraint Lagrange shows in melding the two idioms.

Similarly, Erie on the Park, a steel and glass condominium tower with exterior diagonal bracing in River North, starts as an homage — this time to the nearby John Hancock Center — but becomes something far more interesting and unique. For all their grandeur, there is something a little off-putting about Bruce Graham's larger commissions. There's a heaviness to them — left over from the Brutalist 1960s — that is out of synch with today's drive for ever lighter, more transparent construction. Erie suggests a partially deconstructed Hancock that has been renovated for human inhabitation. Nothing is hidden. The asymmetrical setbacks and sharply angled planes are cutaways that reveal the heart of the building and at the same time create some of the sexiest apartments in the city.

Finally, and most importantly, there is process. For Lagrange, a building's style is determined only after the particulars of its program — its site, use, budget, and neighborhood — have been carefully weighed and analyzed. High-end residential in historic neighborhoods, for example, inevitably tips toward traditional. But irregular sites in changing neighborhoods invite a more modern approach. Erie on the Park, 840 Lake Shore Drive, Park Tower, and the rest demonstrate this commitment in different but compelling ways. On the surface, they differ considerably. And yet, the same process of rigorous analysis that produced one also produced the others. In the end, all provide satisfying solutions for challenging architectural problems.

Lagrange's work over the last 20 years, summarized here, shows an architect keenly aware of both trends in modern culture and the shifting realities of the real estate market. They also demonstrate his tenacity. Many of these projects took years — even decades — to reach fruition. Park Tower, for example, his largest commission to date, took six years from initial meeting to start of construction.

Even more intriguing is Union Station, a building Lagrange has worked on in various capacities since his earliest days as an independent architect. To review the various development schemes for the complex is like watching 20 years of real estate hopes and dreams pass before one's eyes: differing combinations of offices, stores, hotels, and condos are endlessly juggled and re-juggled. The one constant is Lagrange. After completing an initial renovation in the late 1980s, he designed two major additions that were never built. He's now working on a third. What is interesting is to see how his ideas have evolved over time. The current version is by far the boldest and most innovative.

Is Lagrange "Modern?" It's an antique question in a way, left over from an era when American architecture — and Chicago architecture in particular — marched more or less in lockstep under the banner of Mies' "less is more" credo.

A better question may be the one Auguste Perret poses in the epigraph to this essay: Is it eternal? In this regard, Lagrange may have less to fear than many of his more ideologically driven contemporaries. Classicism, in one form or another, has been the foundation of Western architecture for three millennia. In the end, good design is good design, no matter what year or style is being discussed.

"The true aim of art," Perret reminds us, "is to lead us dialectically from satisfaction to satisfaction, until it surpasses mere admiration to reach delight in its purest form." I have found much delight in these buildings.

Next page: Detail, maisonette balustrade, 65 East Goethe

ERIE ON THE PARK

510 West Erie Street
Chicago, Illinois
Year Completed: 2002

Years from now, when historians want to reconstruct what life in Chicago was like in the early years of the 21st century, Erie on the Park may well be a key exhibit. The building is all about the massive transformation and revitalization of the downtown area that occurred in the late 1990s and early 2000s, a period when people—young people in particular—were flocking back to the city to live, work, and play. It's also about Lagrange's triumphant rediscovery of Modernism, a style of architecture he more or less abandoned after leaving Skidmore to begin what became a series of historical investigations. Erie was the first new steel and glass residential tower to be erected in Chicago since the 1960s when buildings such as the John Hancock Center and Lake Point Tower were redefining ideas about downtown living. (More than one critic has observed that Erie in some ways functions as an homage to the Hancock and to its designer, Lagrange's mentor Bruce Graham.) And indeed, part of Erie's considerable charm is the way it at times summons up this earlier period—the Rat Pack era of martinis, Sinatra records on the stereo and bachelor pads with black naugahyde furniture. But the building is much more than an exercise in nostalgia. More than just about any building in Lagrange's oeuvre, Erie is a fabulous object, an illuminated urban stalactite. The jagged, asymmetrical design—a product of its irregular site but also a nod to the Deconstructivist esthetic—represents a step up the evolutionary ladder from the rectilinear heaviness of Lagrange's Skidmore years. It's also a building geared to the young. If 65 East Goethe is where the company CEO lives, Erie is home to the impeccably hip creative director. The finishes are basic, the apartments open and dramatic. The views, of course, are staggering.

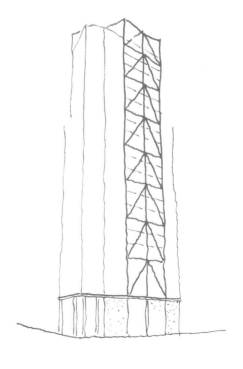

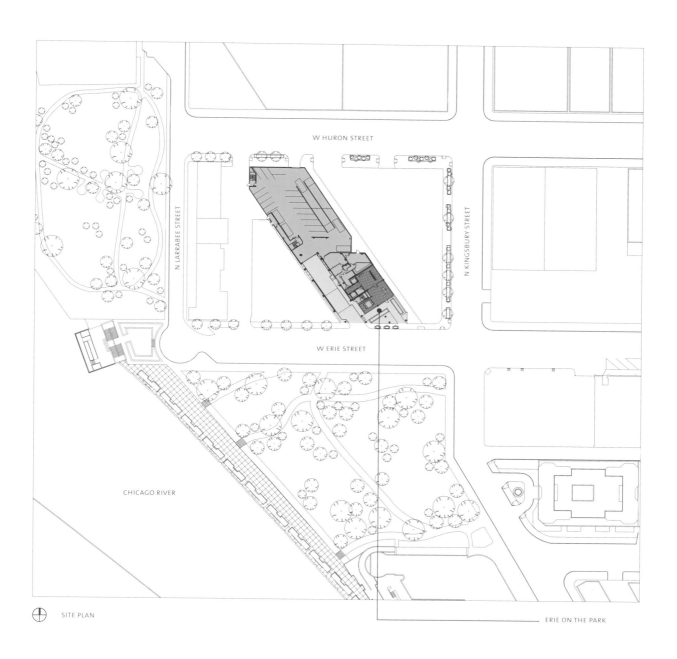

CHICAGO RIVER

W HURON STREET

N LARRABEE STREET

N KINGSBURY STREET

W ERIE STREET

ERIE ON THE PARK

Erie on the Park's challenging site is a 10,000-square-foot parallelogram wedged between two older industrial buildings. The site fronts on a newly created riverfront park.

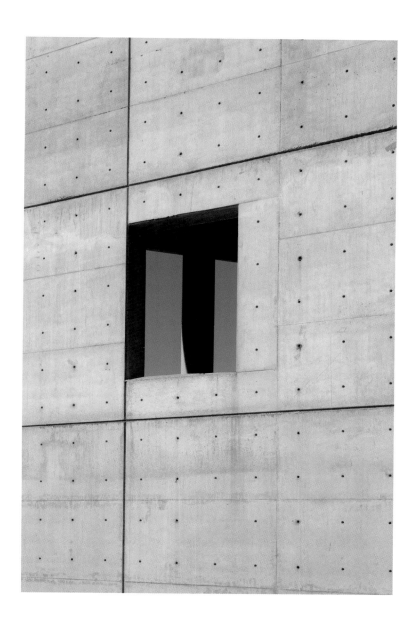

Lucien Lagrange in the lobby of Erie on the Park.

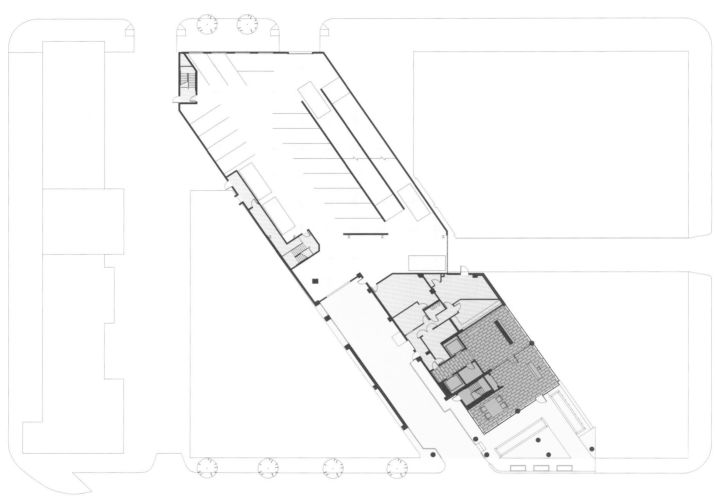

⊕ GROUND LEVEL AND SITE PLAN

The building's ground floor contains a lobby, parking, and service areas. Above that are three additional levels of parking. The 24-story steel and glass tower rises on the southern half of the site.

SITE   SERVICE   LOBBY   CIRCULATION   PARKING   CONDO/HOTEL

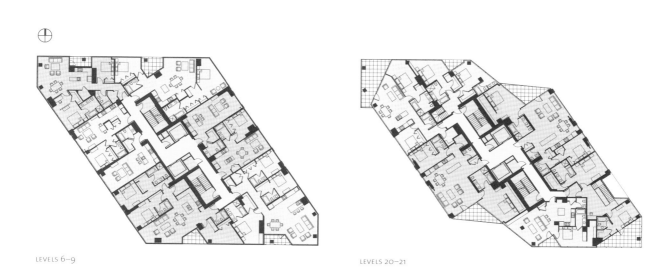

LEVELS 6–9

LEVELS 20–21

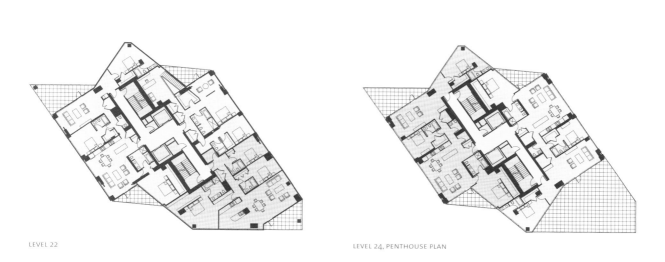

LEVEL 22

LEVEL 24, PENTHOUSE PLAN

As the building rises, apartments and terraces grow larger. There are 18 different apartment floorplans, ranging in size from 600 square feet up to 2,400 square feet. The layouts are open and loft-like with combined kitchen-dining-living spaces and are geared to the building's panoramic views of downtown Chicago.

PARK TOWER

800 North Michigan Avenue
Chicago, Illinois
Year Completed: 2000

Park Tower was Lagrange's big break in terms of commercial acceptance and he poured into it everything he knows and feels about urban living. It's a sexy building—slender, curvaceous and very well accessorized with some of the most elegant Art Deco detailing on Michigan Avenue. At 68 stories, the building also has a complicated program that includes street-level retail, a Park Hyatt Hotel, an elaborate restaurant, 48 floors of residential condominiums, and parking. In addition, an existing two-story landmark façade needed to be preserved and incorporated into the final design. All of this takes place on a fairly small—28,000 square feet—site. The organization is intelligent, with separate entrances and lobbies for the hotel and condominium components. The hotel entrance is on Chicago Avenue and features an automobile drop off shielded by an arching glass canopy. The residential entrance, meanwhile, has a smaller, sunburst canopy and is located around the corner on the much quieter Water Tower Square side. The street-level detailing includes polished black granite window bays and slender bands of smooth and rusticated stone. Inside, too, there are numerous felicitous touches, including a dramatic lobby and a stunning restaurant on the seventh floor with spectacular views of Water Tower Square. The building narrows above the 17th floor in a structurally sophisticated way. At the top, the mansard roof is occupied by a 300-ton tuned mass damper system—one of a handful in the United States—that minimizes building sway caused by the gusty winds off nearby Lake Michigan.

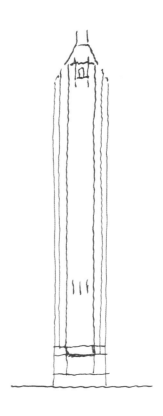

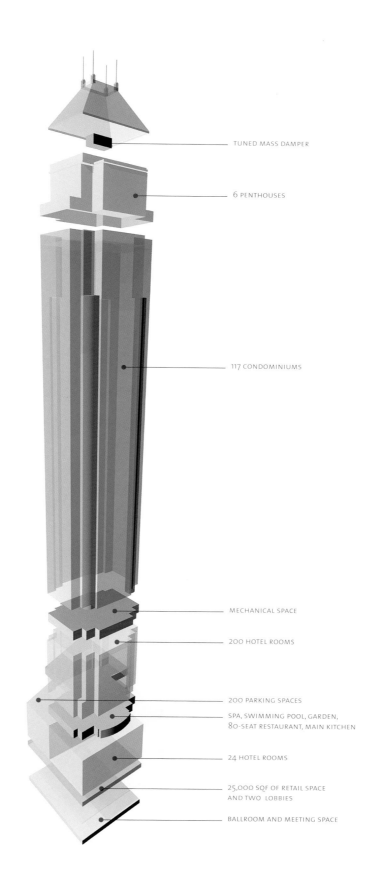

TUNED MASS DAMPER

6 PENTHOUSES

117 CONDOMINIUMS

MECHANICAL SPACE

200 HOTEL ROOMS

200 PARKING SPACES

SPA, SWIMMING POOL, GARDEN,
80-SEAT RESTAURANT, MAIN KITCHEN

24 HOTEL ROOMS

25,000 SQF OF RETAIL SPACE
AND TWO LOBBIES

BALLROOM AND MEETING SPACE

At 68 stories, Park Tower is one of the tallest buildings in downtown Chicago. The seven-story base includes separate lobbies for the hotel and residential components of the building as well as 25,000 square feet of retail space. The upper floors contain 224 hotel rooms, a restaurant, a spa, and 123 condominiums.

Above: The seventh-floor health club has a lap pool with large windows looking out over the city. Next page: The terrace of the top floor penthouse has an unobstructed view of Lake Michigan.

Above: The lobby of the Park Hyatt Hotel is defined by the four large structural columns that rise up through the center of the building. Next page: A steel and glass staircase in the lobby leads to the ballroom.

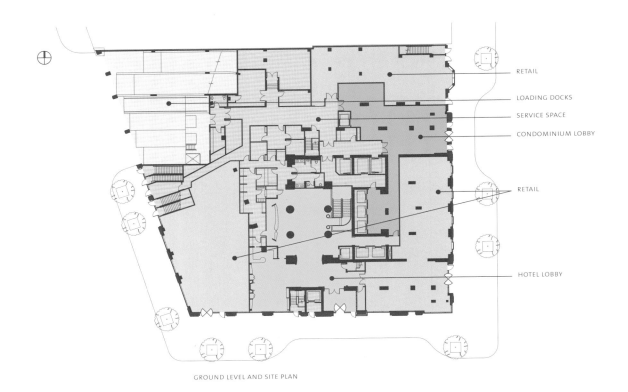

RETAIL

LOADING DOCKS

SERVICE SPACE

CONDOMINIUM LOBBY

RETAIL

HOTEL LOBBY

GROUND LEVEL AND SITE PLAN

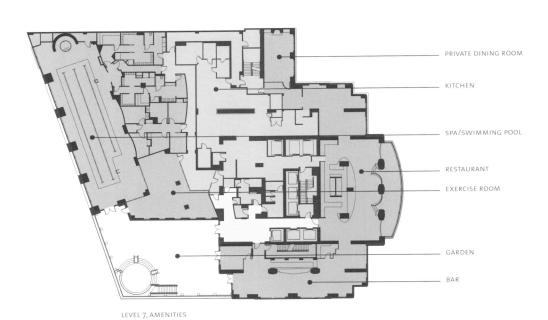

PRIVATE DINING ROOM

KITCHEN

SPA/SWIMMING POOL

RESTAURANT

EXERCISE ROOM

GARDEN

BAR

LEVEL 7, AMENITIES

Top: Park Tower's first floor includes separate lobbies for the hotel and condominium components of the building along with retail space and service areas.
Bottom: The seventh floor includes a restaurant and bar with an elaborate bay window looking out on Water Tower Square, a health club with a lap pool as well as a landscaped garden used for dining and special events.

SERVICE	LOBBY	CIRCULATION	PARKING	RETAIL	AMENITIES
CONDO/HOTEL	PENTHOUSE				

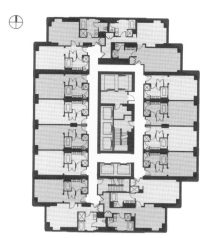

TYPICAL HOTEL PLAN

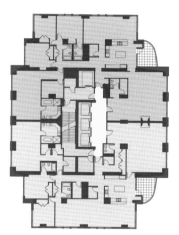

TYPICAL RESIDENTIAL PLAN

LEVEL 67, TYPICAL PENTHOUSE PLAN

Top: Park Tower's hotel rooms average 450 square feet and surround a central core containing elevators and utilities. Middle: Residential condominiums all have east-facing living rooms and balconies that provide unobstructed views of Lake Michigan. Bottom: The building's upper floors are occupied by six full floor penthouses that have about 6,700 square feet of living space.

LEVEL 61, PENTHOUSE PLAN

Previous page and above: The layout of this ultra-modern penthouse is open and accessible with a large east-facing living room, three bedrooms, a master bath with a deluxe double shower, and a mini-gymnasium. Ceiling heights are 13 feet.

SERVICE   PENTHOUSE

SIXTY-FIVE EAST GOETHE

65 East Goethe Street
Chicago, Illinois
Year Completed: 2002

Neither a slavish copy nor a Post Modern pastiche, Sixty-Five East Goethe is something far more interesting and ambitious: a serious attempt to re-introduce Classicism to Chicago, a city with a formidable — though often overlooked — Classical legacy. Sixty-Five has a crisply articulated limestone façade and is accessorized with some of the finest custom ironwork in the city. The latter is crucial to the building's impact. Classicism balances strength and delicacy. The numerous filigreed wrought iron grills and balustrades — not to mention the iron picket fence that surrounds the property — add charm and buoyancy to the building's cliff-like form. Like all of Lagrange's best residential work, Sixty-Five is about the romance of city life. One can imagine walking by the building at twilight, staring up into the glowing, high-ceilinged rooms and wondering about the life that goes on in there. In form, the building resembles a slightly oversized traditional Parisian "hotel particulier." The 24 apartments range in size from 2,000 square feet up to about 10,000 square feet. Among the amenities are a rooftop garden with a view of Lake Michigan as well as a landscaped inner courtyard. Sixty-Five has the feel of something Lagrange has wanted to do for a long time. It's nostalgic without being precious and surprisingly muscular. It is, all in all, one of his most personal projects.

Previous page: The front entrance's elaborate iron grill. Above: A balustrade for one of the building's maisonette apartments.

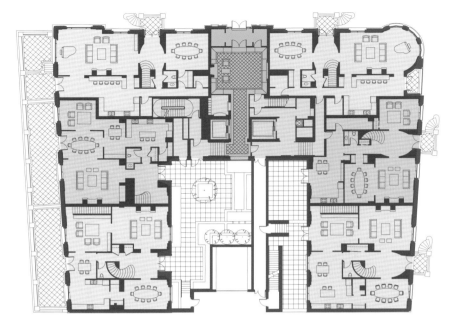

GROUND LEVEL

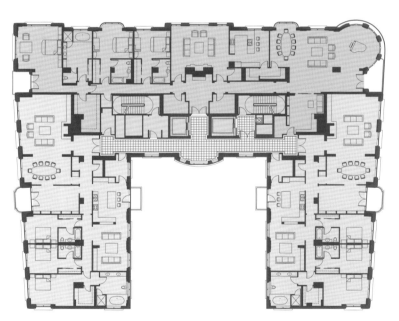

TYPICAL RESIDENTIAL PLAN

Top: In addition to the lobby, 65 East Goethe's first floor includes six duplex maisonettes, four of which have separate street-level entrances. Bottom: The upper floors have three apartments that range in size from 3,500 square feet to 5,000 square feet. All units have at least one balcony. The footprint of 65 East Goethe, following the tradition of Parisian "hotel particuliers," is slightly irregular as it is built out to the property line on all sides in an effort to capture as much square footage as possible.

SERVICE   LOBBY   CIRCULATION   CONDO

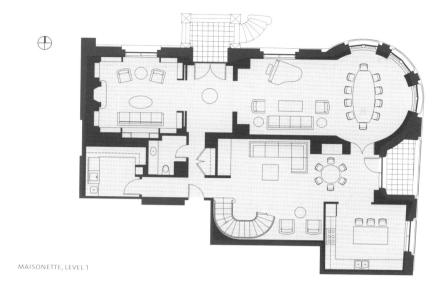

MAISONETTE, LEVEL 1

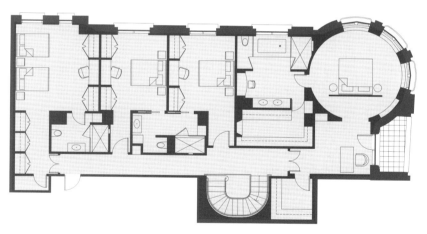

MAISONETTE, LEVEL 2

This two-story, 4,520-square-foot maisonette has a street-level entrance and balconies on both levels. The rounded corner turret allows for a variety of uses. On the first level (top), it serves as a dining room. On the second, it provides a unique focal point to the master bedroom suite. The unit also contains three other bedrooms on the second level including a second master suite.

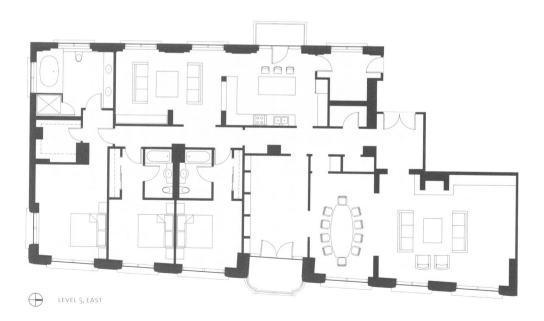

⊕ LEVEL 5, EAST

This three-bedroom, 3,580-square-foot condominium features a large formal living room and dining room plus an eat-in kitchen. The rooms open off a gallery that runs the length of the apartment. The apartment has two balconies, one off the library facing the street and a second off the kitchen that overlooks the interior courtyard.

CONDO

1712 South Prairie Avenue
Chicago, Illinois
Scheduled Completion Date: 2010

Lagrange compares these two unusually cantilevered condominium towers to tango dancers who bend away from each other at the waist. At their respective peaks, the towers are 20 feet off center, enough to give them an exciting sculptural presence in a neighborhood dominated by traditional glass box apartment buildings. X/O is an outgrowth of an earlier unbuilt project in Dubai where Lagrange first began experimenting with a more abstract approach to design. The towers are connected by a six-story base containing lobbies and a large, 15,000-square-foot health club. The base has a fritted concrete façade along with a 28,000-square-foot green roof that functions as a garden for the project as a whole. The complex also includes a row of townhouses along the Prairie Avenue frontage of the site. The towers are constructed of reinforced concrete with glass curtain walls. The varied fenestration reflects the layout of the apartments within. The North Tower, the taller of the two, contains 270 units while the South Tower contains 210 units.

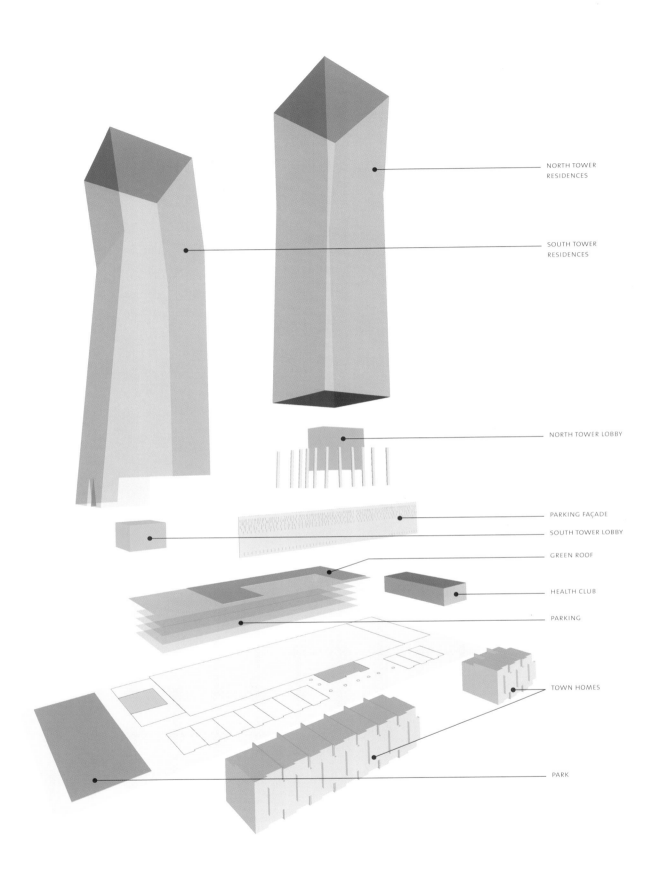

NORTH TOWER
RESIDENCES

SOUTH TOWER
RESIDENCES

NORTH TOWER LOBBY

PARKING FAÇADE

SOUTH TOWER LOBBY

GREEN ROOF

HEALTH CLUB

PARKING

TOWN HOMES

PARK

X/O's two unusually cantilevered towers rest on a six-story base with a fritted façade containing lobbies and parking. The base has a green roof that also serves as a garden for the residents. Just north of the base is a health club and along the front of the 2-acre site is a row of 10 townhouses.

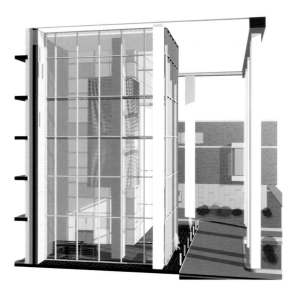

Above: The north tower has a 60-foot lobby behind a portico of exposed structural piers. Next page: The lobby of the south tower opens onto a small park.

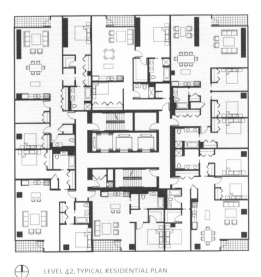

LEVEL 42, TYPICAL RESIDENTIAL PLAN

Although the basic footprint remains consistent, the individual floorplans change continually due to the bending of the towers. A typical floor has six units, each with its own balcony off the living room. The layouts are open to maximize both light and views from the floor-to-ceiling windows. The units are grouped around a central utility core and noise from the elevator shafts is buffered by placing them between stairwells.

SITE   SERVICE   LOBBY   CIRCULATION   PARKING   AMENITIES   CONDO/HOTEL

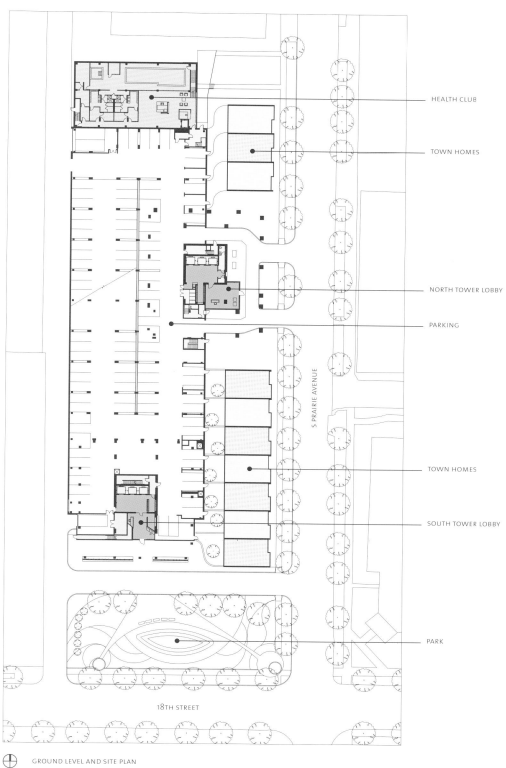

HEALTH CLUB

TOWN HOMES

NORTH TOWER LOBBY

PARKING

S PRAIRIE AVENUE

TOWN HOMES

SOUTH TOWER LOBBY

PARK

18TH STREET

GROUND LEVEL AND SITE PLAN

X/O is located just north of the Prairie Avenue Historic District, a block of two- and three-story 19th-century mansions that includes H.H. Richardson's Glessner House. By aligning the two towers along the rear of the 92,000-square-foot site and behind a row of three-story townhouses, the low-rise nature of the original streetwall is maintained.

KINGSBURY ON THE PARK

653 North Kingsbury Street
Chicago, Illinois
Year Completed: 2003

Like Erie on the Park, its fraternal twin across the street, Kingsbury on the
Park appears light and flexible. Both buildings seem like they could have been
snapped together out of kits. There's a playful quality to them. The two are the
first new steel and glass residential buildings to be erected in Chicago since
the 1960s. Since then, for reasons of cost, reinforced concrete has become the
norm. Kingsbury and Erie demonstrate what has been lost in the process.
Steel opens up a world of design options. Floor-to-ceiling windows? No
problem. Column-less floorplans? Check. Kingsbury has a more regular site
than Erie, which allows for a more regular floorplan. The result is a 23-story
tower atop a 6-story base. In order to add interest to what would otherwise
be a fairly traditional glass box, Lagrange plays a number of lively games with
the building's fenestration, particularly at the summit where the top two
bays on either side of the square are left open. Kingsbury's most pronounced
architectural feature, however, are its balconies, some of which are recessed
but most of which are attached to the building by tiers of vertical steel trusses.
The trusses have an erector set quality to them. From certain angles, they
give the building an unfinished look that is consistent with the emerging
Deconstructivist esthetic. Erie and Kingsbury also have identical structural
systems consisting of three-story inverted-v megabraces. The difference is
that Erie's are on the exterior while Kingsbury's rise up through the center
core of the building.

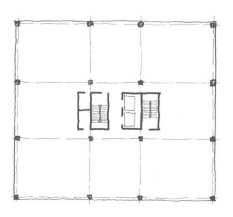

Kingsbury on the Park's drop-off and lobby on Kingsbury Street.

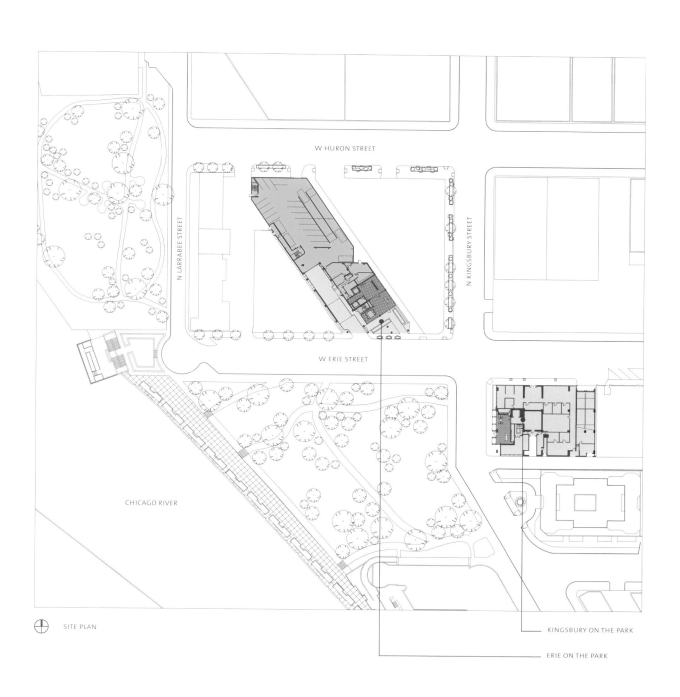

SITE PLAN

W HURON STREET

N LARRABEE STREET

N KINGSBURY STREET

W ERIE STREET

CHICAGO RIVER

KINGSBURY ON THE PARK

ERIE ON THE PARK

Kingsbury on the Park is located diagonally across the street from Erie on the Park. Both buildings front on a newly created riverfront park.

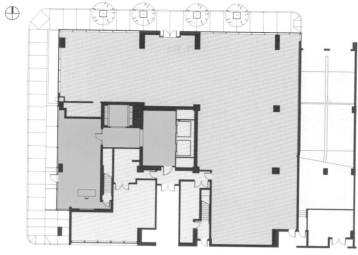

GROUND LEVEL

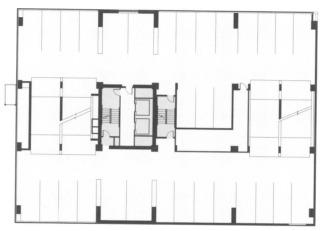

LEVELS 3–5, PARKING

LEVEL 18, TYPICAL RESIDENTIAL PLAN

Top: Kingsbury on the Park's ground level includes a drop off and lobby on Kingsbury Street and 6,543 square feet of retail space. Middle: The six-story base contains 169 parking spaces. Bottom: A typical floor has six apartments, a mix of one- and two-bedroom units. All units have at least one balcony.

SERVICE   LOBBY   CIRCULATION   PARKING   AMENITIES   CONDO

LEVEL 25, PENTHOUSE PLAN

The 2,973-square-foot penthouse depicted here and on the following pages is one of three top-floor units. The apartment includes four bedrooms and a spacious terrace. The photograph above is taken from the unit's terrace.

PENTHOUSE

PARK KINGSBURY

Chicago, Illinois

Located adjacent to Erie on the Park and across the street from Kingsbury on the Park, Park Kingsbury incorporates elements of both buildings while establishing its own unique presence on the skyline. Both Erie and Kingsbury are steel and glass buildings with all the lightness and flexibility those materials imply. Park Kingsbury, however—following the almost universal trend of new condominium buildings in recent years—is made of reinforced concrete. Lagrange's challenge, then, was to design something that would sustain the qualities of those earlier buildings while using a very different material. The elevations are a scrambled checkerboard of glass and concrete panels—a dash of early-1960s graphic design. It's all pattern. Weight is not a factor. All three buildings have matching concrete and glass bases. Like Erie, Park Kingsbury has an irregular site—basically a 24,380-square-foot abbreviated triangle—that influenced the ultimate form of the tower. That form is an irregular hexagon. The building is steps away from Erie but due to careful siting, both buildings enjoy mainly uninterrupted views from their floor-to-ceiling windows. The tower rises 28 stories and contains 165 condominiums.

SITE PLAN

KINGSBURY ON THE PARK

PARK KINGSBURY

ERIE ON THE PARK

W HURON STREET

N LARRABEE STREET

N KINGSBURY STREET

W ERIE STREET

CHICAGO RIVER

Park Kingsbury's irregular 24,380-square-foot site is adjacent to Erie on the Park and diagonally across the street from Kingsbury on the Park. All border on a newly created riverfront park. The 28-story tower occupies less than half of the property and is angled so that units in both Park Kingsbury and Erie on the Park have mainly unobstructed views.

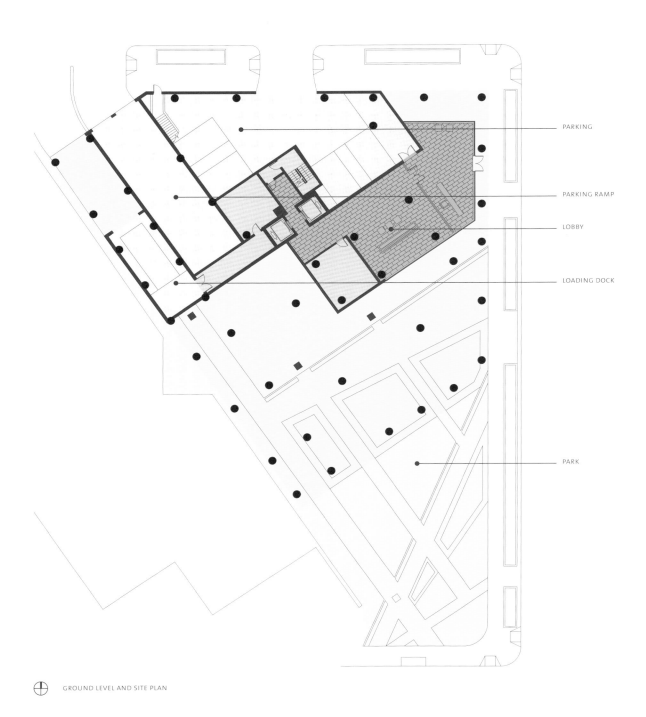

PARKING

PARKING RAMP

LOBBY

LOADING DOCK

PARK

⊕ GROUND LEVEL AND SITE PLAN

Park Kingsbury's site is an irregular triangle with the tower and six-story base located along the northern periphery and with a landscaped plaza leading down to a newly created riverfront park.

SITE   SERVICE   LOBBY   CIRCULATION   PARKING   CONDO

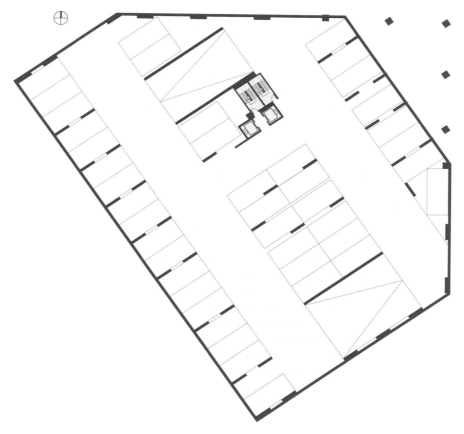

LEVELS 2–5, PARKING

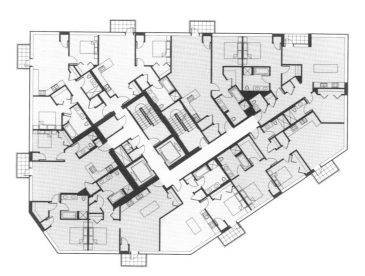

LEVEL 8, TYPICAL RESIDENTIAL PLAN

Top: Levels two through five are used for parking. Bottom: A typical floor has eight apartments arranged along an L-shaped corridor. The units range in size from 700 square feet to 1,622 square feet and no two layouts are identical.

PLAZA ESCADA

840 North Michigan Avenue
Chicago, Illinois
Year Completed: 1992

Plaza Escada was the first new building Lagrange designed as an independent architect and it signaled a major shift in his approach. Believing that the Modernism of the 1970s and early 80s had reached a dead end, he looked to the past for fresh inspiration. The result was this handsome Classically inspired retail structure located across from Water Tower Place Mall. At the time, it was considered a daring, even controversial, choice. Lagrange's thinking, however, was that Michigan Avenue had a varied architectural heritage that included everything from the Beaux Arts richness of the Wrigley Building to the Modernist grandeur of Bruce Graham's Hancock Building. No one style predominated. The building also needed to reflect the fact that the street is the traditional home of the city's finest carriage trade merchants. The details—the ornamental columns around the doorway, the clock tower with its mansard roof—are carefully worked out. The loading docks, which are located on Chestnut Street, are another grace note; they are concealed behind what appears to be the façade of a brick roughhouse. The building anchors its corner well, neither a wallflower nor a too-insistent presence on a street with more than its share of both.

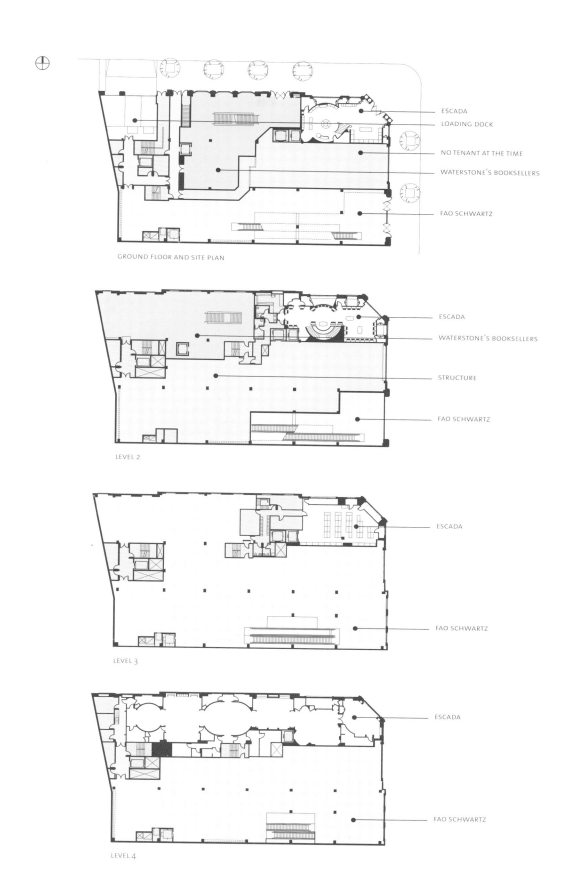

GROUND FLOOR AND SITE PLAN

ESCADA
LOADING DOCK
NO TENANT AT THE TIME
WATERSTONE'S BOOKSELLERS
FAO SCHWARTZ

LEVEL 2

ESCADA
WATERSTONE'S BOOKSELLERS
STRUCTURE
FAO SCHWARTZ

LEVEL 3

ESCADA
FAO SCHWARTZ

LEVEL 4

ESCADA
FAO SCHWARTZ

Plaza Escada was designed for retail tenants who wanted street-level entrances but otherwise had widely varying space requirements. The loading docks for all four spaces are at the northwest corner and are concealed behind a façade resembling a brick rowhouse.

SERVICE   CIRCULATION   PARKING   RETAIL

EIGHT-FORTY NORTH LAKE SHORE DRIVE

840 North Lake Shore Drive
Chicago, Illinois
Year Completed: 2003

Lagrange conceived of 840 Lake Shore Drive as the exclamation point at the end of a four-block row of historic — primarily pre-war — residential buildings that starts at Michigan Avenue and extends east and south to Pearson Street. It includes the one-block East Lake Shore Drive historic district, which is generally considered the city's most exclusive address, as well as 860 and 880 Lake Shore Drive, two early steel and glass apartment buildings designed by Mies van der Rohe. Lagrange cites architect Benjamin Marshall's 1908 Blackstone Hotel on Michigan Avenue as the inspiration for 840's beautifully rendered Second Empire roof. The building also has something in common with the Classically inspired Modernism Philip Johnson, Edward Durrell Stone and other architects were practicing in the 1960s and also with Johnson's much later Sony Building in New York. Both Sony and 840 have roofs that are the equivalent of wearing a really smashing hat to an otherwise staid garden party. In many ways, 840 has the grace and form of a classic 1920s residential building. But there are some key differences. For one, 840 is quite a bit taller and more angular than those earlier buildings. It soars. It's also simpler. In addition to the roof, the main design element is a large glass turret at the corner of Lake Shore Drive and Pearson Street topped by an illuminated lantern. Corner turrets are a Chicago tradition, of course, starting with Louis Sullivan's Carson Pirie Scott department store building. (The turret also creates dramatic interior spaces.) Eight-forty's fenestration is lively but contained. There are three tiers of balconies on the building's south façade, two of which are recessed while the third projects slightly. The balconies never overwhelm the building. Rather, given the building's height, they provide needed weight and definition. For all the outré glamour of the building's roof and turret, the overall effect is one of dignity and restraint.

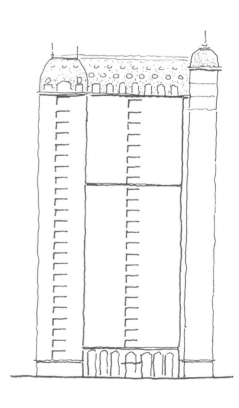

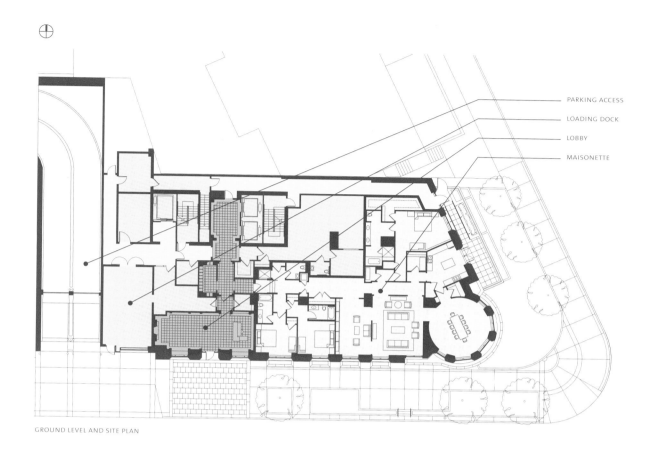

PARKING ACCESS

LOADING DOCK

LOBBY

MAISONETTE

GROUND LEVEL AND SITE PLAN

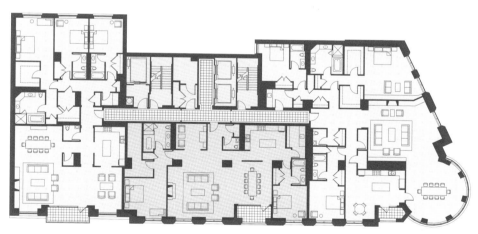

LEVELS 21–24, TYPICAL RESIDENTIAL PLAN

Top: The building's slightly irregular footprint follows the angle of Lake Shore Drive. In addition to the lobby and office areas the ground floor also includes a 4,500-square-foot maisonette apartment with a street-level entrance. Bottom: The building's upper floors contain three apartments per floor, each with its own balcony and ranging in size from 2,100 square feet to 4,300 square feet.

SERVICE   LOBBY   CIRCULATION   PARKING   CONDO/HOTEL

This full-floor, 9,700-square-foot condominium was designed as a pied-à-terre for a couple who needed space for business entertaining and also for fundraising events for various cultural and charitable organizations. The rooms mainly open off a 100-foot-long gallery that runs the length of the apartment and include, among other spaces, an expansive living room and dining room, two powder rooms, a catering pantry, a billiard room, and a media center. The apartment also has three bedrooms including a master suite with large his and hers bathrooms.

SERVICE   CIRCULATION   CONDO/HOTEL

DUBAI TOWER STUDY

Dubai, United Arab Emirates

This project—two unusually faceted towers on a 1.3-acre site—was Lagrange's first experiment with the kind of computer-aided, forward-looking design the firm has subsequently employed for X/O and a number of other structures. Lagrange has stated that the lack of any obvious urban context in Dubai encouraged him to utilize a more purely abstract approach to design. The program called for two buildings, one containing residential units and one for offices. The former has 126 apartments that range in size from 880 to 1,020 square feet. Total square footage is 210,000 square feet. The office floorplates are 6,000 square feet and total square footage is 168,000 square feet.

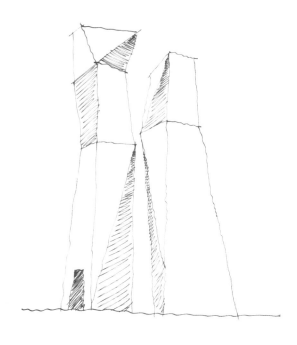

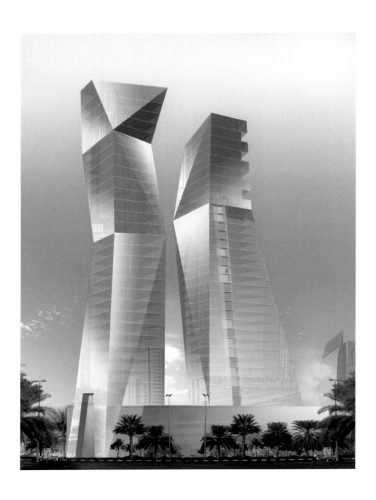

Alternative renderings for the Dubai Tower Study
explored different sculptural solutions while retaining
the basic two-tower concept.

ONE SEVENTY FIVE WEST JACKSON

175 West Jackson Boulevard
Chicago, Illinois
Year Completed: 2001

At 1.8 million square feet, 175 West Jackson is Lagrange's largest historic renovation project to date. It also has some of his most exuberant interior work. The building—a 21-story Neo-Classical structure sheathed in gleaming white terra cotta—occupies a square block in the heart of Chicago's financial district. The building dates from 1912 and was designed by Daniel Burnham. It doubled in size in 1928 when a seamless addition by Burnham's successor firm, Graham Anderson Probst and White, was completed. For many years, 175—originally the Insurance Exchange Building—was the city's largest office building. By the early 1990s, however, when it was acquired by a New York real estate firm, the building had fallen into a twilight zone of deferred maintenance and falling occupancy levels. Lagrange's mandate was to restore the facility to its original status as a Class A office property. The transformation starts on the sidewalk where a drab one-story entryway has been reconfigured as a two-story atrium blooming with light and color. The effect is particularly striking at night when—from the street—it appears an illuminated crystal box has been inserted into the base of the building. The complex has two central light courts, one of which had been closed off since the 1950s. Lagrange reopened the latter to spectacular effect. A new three-story skylight—supported by dramatic spider-like constructions in the four corners of the space—was installed, as were rich cherry wood accents and metal storefronts. The building also contains numerous custom-designed stainless steel accents and fixtures, such as elevator doors, balustrades, and chandeliers. In addition, the building's 4,400 windows have been replaced and its terra cotta façade has been thoroughly scrubbed and repaired. Finally, one of the building's sub-basements has been transformed into a 200-car parking garage. In 2001, the Chicago Commercial Real Estate Awards honored 175 as Redevelopment of the Year.

Above: The renovation included creating a new two-story lobby and installing a steel and glass canopy over the entrance. Next page: The new lobby features a multi-colored marble floor and stainless steel planters and chandeliers.

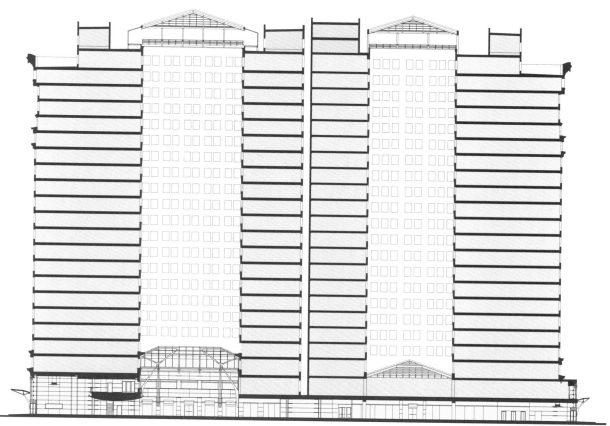

SECTION PLAN

The defining features of 175 West Jackson are the two central light wells. The north well (left) originally had been closed off for many years. The highlight of the renovation involved reopening the north well, installing a three-story skylight, and converting the newly created atrium into a retail area.

SERVICE   CIRCULATION   OFFICE

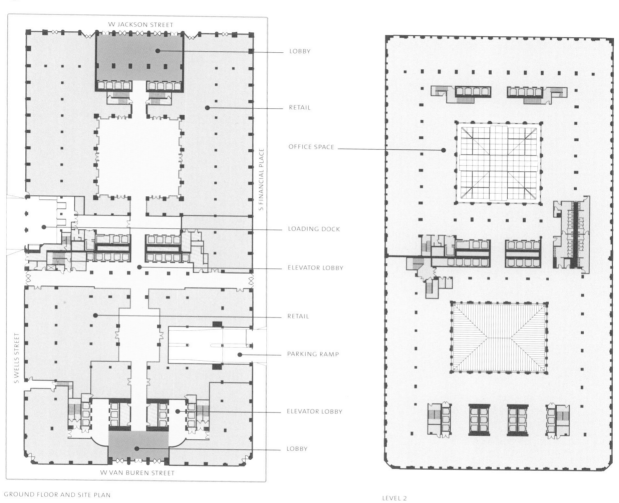

W JACKSON STREET

LOBBY

RETAIL

S FINANCIAL PLACE

LOADING DOCK

ELEVATOR LOBBY

RETAIL

S WELLS STREET

PARKING RAMP

ELEVATOR LOBBY

LOBBY

W VAN BUREN STREET

GROUND FLOOR AND SITE PLAN

OFFICE SPACE

LEVEL 2

Left: The renovation retained the original ground-level circulation pattern while enlarging the main lobby and substantially increasing retail space.
Right: A typical office floor.

| SERVICE | LOBBY | CIRCULATION | PARKING | OFFICE | RETAIL | AMENITIES |

BLUE CHIP CASINO HOTEL

2 Easy Street
Michigan City, Indiana
Scheduled Completion Date: 2009

Blue Chip, a hotel and gambling casino about an hour east of Chicago in
a resort community on Lake Michigan, was looking to upgrade its image
and become more of a weekend destination when it hired Lagrange to
renovate its existing facility and add a new wing consisting of a 300-room
hotel and a 15,000-square-foot ballroom. The curvilinear hotel tower taps
into the current fascination with 1960s Rat Pack glamour. Sheathed in
blue-green glass and rising 23 stories, it suggests a more streamlined
version of early Las Vegas gambling meccas like the Sands and the Stardust
hotels. Lagrange also reoriented several roads to smooth out circulation
and improved the landscaping.

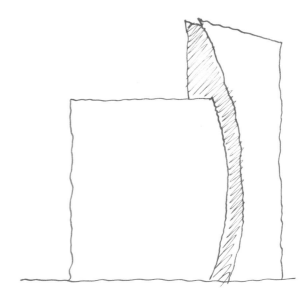

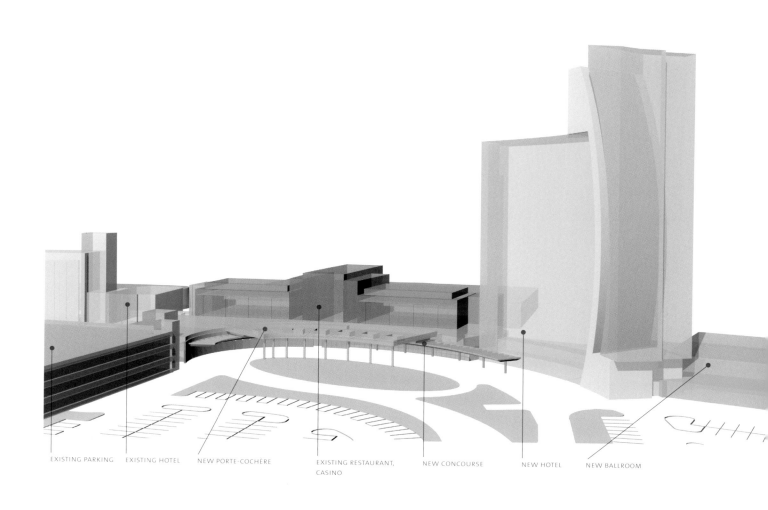

EXISTING PARKING   EXISTING HOTEL   NEW PORTE-COCHÈRE   EXISTING RESTAURANT,   NEW CONCOURSE   NEW HOTEL   NEW BALLROOM
                                                           CASINO

The renovation more than doubles the original square footage of the complex and includes a greatly enlarged porte-cochère entryway and a 23-story hotel tower with an adjacent ballroom.

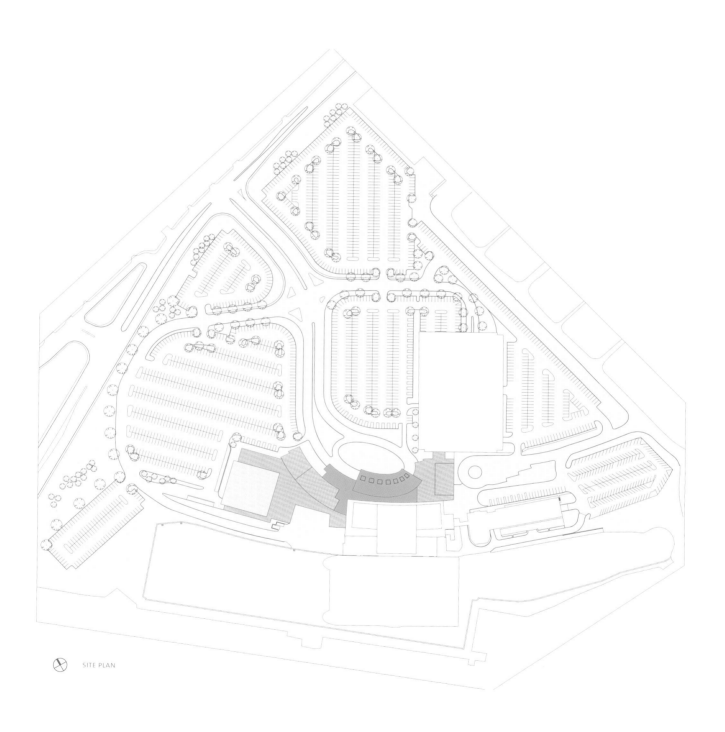

⊕ SITE PLAN

New landscaping and reconfigured roadways create a resort-like feel not present in the original campus. In addition, a traffic oval across from the main entrance provides a sense of arrival while at the same time smoothing out circulation.

SITE   LOBBY   AMENITIES   HOTEL   EXISTING STRUCTURES   CONFERENCE/BALLROOM

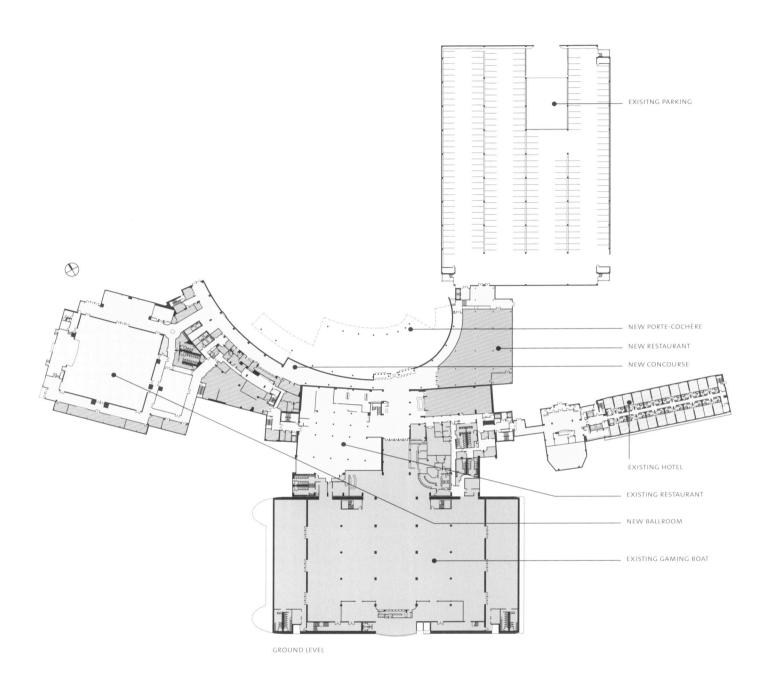

EXISITNG PARKING

NEW PORTE-COCHÈRE

NEW RESTAURANT

NEW CONCOURSE

EXISTING HOTEL

EXISTING RESTAURANT

NEW BALLROOM

EXISTING GAMING BOAT

GROUND LEVEL

The new hotel tower and ballroom transforms the property into a resort suitable for weekend stays and business meetings. The addition also streamlines circulation between the different elements—hotel, casino, ballroom, and parking—and raises the profile of the hospitality component.

SERVICE   CIRCULATION   PARKING   RETAIL   AMENITIES   HOTEL   CONFERENCE/BALLROOM

LEVEL 2, SPA PLAN

LEVELS 3–17, TYPICAL HOTEL PLAN

LEVELS 20–21, TYPICAL HOTEL PLAN

Top: The second floor contains a full service spa and fitness center that includes large whirlpools, massage facilities, and a hair salon. Middle: The upper floors contain "high-roller" suites of 1,000 square feet or more. Bottom: A typical floor has 19 rooms that average between 430 and 1,000 square feet.

STEELTOWN RESIDENCES

Chicago, Illinois

Steeltown—a mixed-use retail and condominium project in a gentrifying residential neighborhood—is notable for the way it confronts an extremely challenging site and transforms it into a desirable urban location. The irregular 39,000-square-foot lot is bordered on two sides by elevated railroad tracks while the remaining two sides front on busy urban thoroughfares. The surrounding neighborhood is a mix of low-rise single- and multi-family residences interspersed with a number of small industrial buildings dating from the turn of the century. Most of the latter have been or are in the process of being converted to lofts. Lagrange's solution is a five-story Bauhaus-influenced building that—with its exposed steel frame and floor-to-ceiling windows—openly celebrates the area's industrial past. The project has 14,5000 square feet of retail space on the first floor and 34 condominiums overhead. The condominiums are a mix of one- and two-bedroom apartments that range in size from about 900 square feet to 1,500 square feet and are geared to young professionals. The units are aligned along a single-loaded corridor in order to minimize noise from the nearby train tracks. Setbacks at one end of the building provide expansive terraces for the two-bedroom units. The one-bedroom units all have front-facing balconies with brightly colored steel divider panels that reinforce the residential nature of the project.

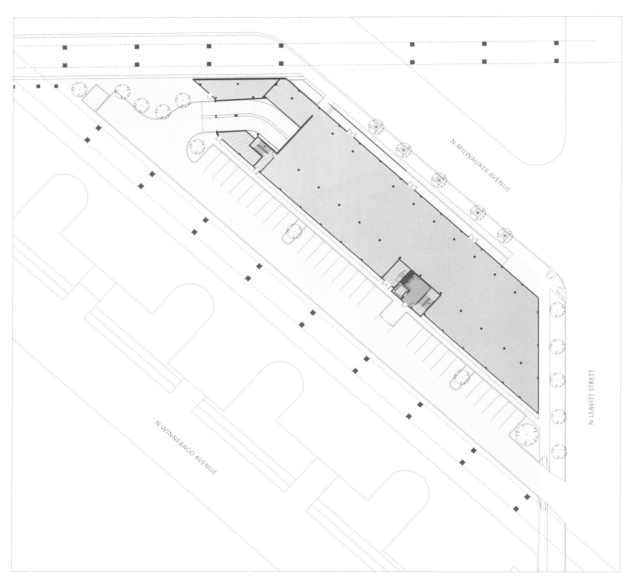

⊕ GROUND LEVEL AND SITE PLAN

Steeltown's 39,000-square-foot site is surrounded on two sides by railroad tracks. The ground floor consists of 14,389 square feet of retail space. The project also includes underground parking.

SITE   SERVICE   LOBBY   CIRCULATION   PARKING   RETAIL   CONDO

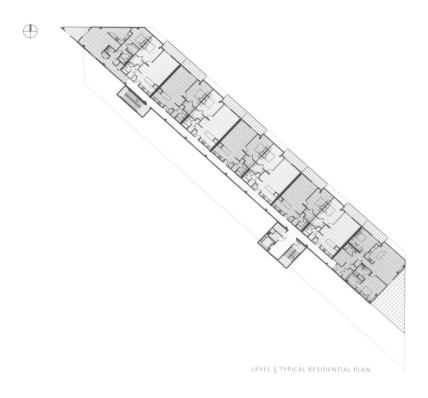

LEVEL 3, TYPICAL RESIDENTIAL PLAN

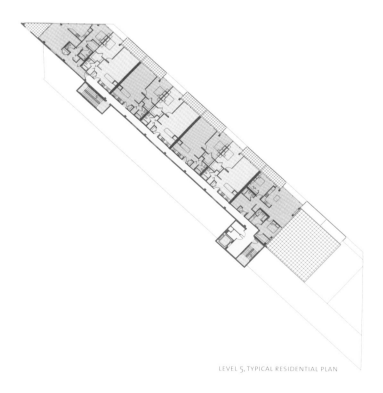

LEVEL 5, TYPICAL RESIDENTIAL PLAN

The apartments are aligned along a single-loaded corridor with a windowless back wall in order to minimize noise from the nearby railroad tracks. All units have either a balcony or a terrace.

HARD ROCK HOTEL

230 North Michigan Avenue
Chicago, Illinois
Year Completed: 2004

For sheer complexity, few projects equal Lagrange's conversion of the landmark Carbide and Carbon Building into a 383-room Hard Rock Hotel. The 38-story building was designed by Burnham Brothers in 1929 as a headquarters for the company that invented the Ever-Ready battery and is considered one of the city's most important Art Deco structures. (Local legend has it that the gilded pinnacle was modeled after an exploding champagne bottle.) The hotel required amenities—such as a restaurant, bar, ballroom, and meeting rooms—not present in the existing building. There were also a number of landmark spaces and details—including a stunning lobby on Michigan Avenue—that needed to be preserved. In addition, the elevators needed to be reconfigured and a fire stair added. Lagrange's solution included constructing a new three-story addition on Michigan Avenue to house the hotel's bar, restaurant, and ballroom. The addition—in keeping with Hard Rock's progressive image—has a Modern façade done in polished black granite and glass and with nickel hardware that harmonizes with the older building. Lagrange also shifted the building's main entrance from Michigan Avenue to Water Street and carved out a new lobby in what had been retail space along the building's north façade. Meanwhile, the vintage interior spaces were meticulously restored. The highlight is undoubtedly the original main lobby on Michigan Avenue with its Parisian-inspired frosted glass panels and light fixtures and burnished brass hardware and balustrades. On the exterior, about 10 percent of the building's green terra cotta tiles had to be replaced. The rest needed to be variously repaired and cleaned. In addition, new historically accurate double-hung windows were installed.

Above and next page: A new entrance and lobby were created along the north side of the original building.

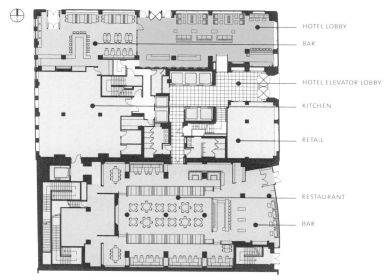

HOTEL LOBBY

BAR

HOTEL ELEVATOR LOBBY

KITCHEN

RETAIL

RESTAURANT

BAR

GROUND LEVEL

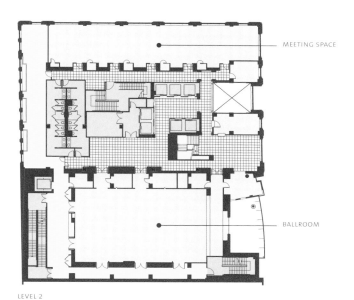

MEETING SPACE

BALLROOM

LEVEL 2

TYPICAL TOWER HOTEL PLAN

Top: A new entrance and lobby were created on the Water Street side of the original building. The three-story addition includes a restaurant and bar and nearly doubles the original footprint of the facility to 18,973 square feet. Middle: The upper floors of the addition are occupied by a 2,917-square-foot ballroom. Bottom: Hotel rooms average 350 square feet in the 14-story tower.

SERVICE   LOBBY   CIRCULATION   AMENITIES   CONDO/HOTEL   CONFERENCE/BALLROOM

TWO ZERO EIGHT SOUTH LASALLE

208 South LaSalle Street
Chicago, Illinois
Scheduled Completion Date: 2009

This massive — one-million-square-foot — office building dates from the
1920s and has a prime location a block north of the Chicago Board of Trade.
For years, the facility housed various financial firms and the base includes
a grand two-story banking hall ringed with Classical columns. Recently,
the owner decided to redevelop the first 12 of the building's 21 floors into
a 600-plus-room luxury hotel with extensive meeting and ballroom space.
Lagrange's plan calls for creating a new entrance and lobby for the hotel
around the corner on Adams Street. In addition, the banking hall will be
reconfigured into two ballrooms while retaining as much of the original
detailing as possible. The hotel rooms, meanwhile, will include a mix of
single rooms and luxury suites.

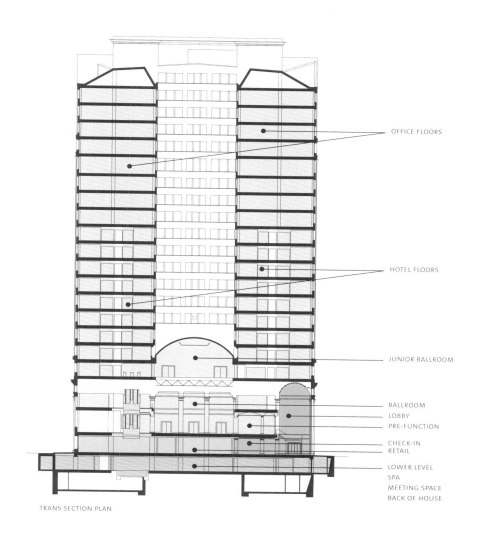

OFFICE FLOORS

HOTEL FLOORS

JUNIOR BALLROOM

BALLROOM
LOBBY
PRE-FUNCTION

CHECK-IN
RETAIL

LOWER LEVEL
SPA
MEETING SPACE
BACK OF HOUSE

TRANS SECTION PLAN

Previous page: The hotel's new entrance and lobby on Adams Street. Above: The hotel's lobby and ballrooms were carved out of space formerly occupied by a banking hall.

SERVICE   LOBBY   CIRCULATION   OFFICE   RETAIL   AMENITIES

CONDO/HOTEL   CONFERENCE/BALLROOM

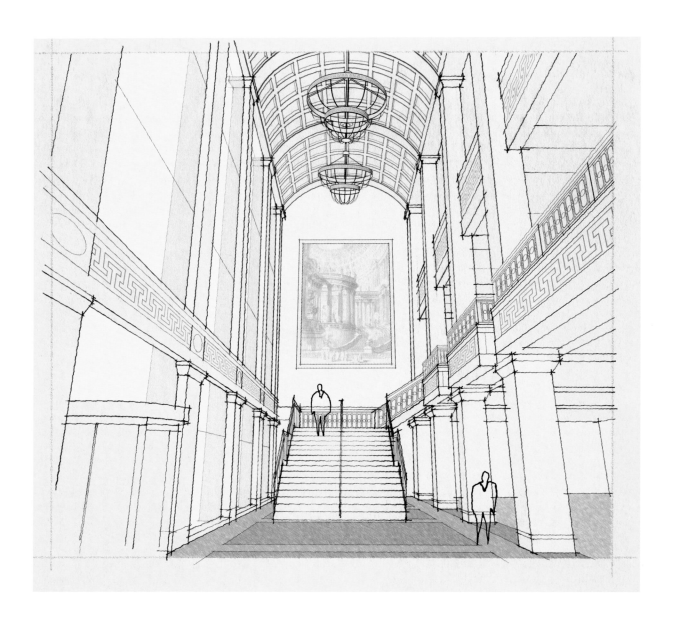

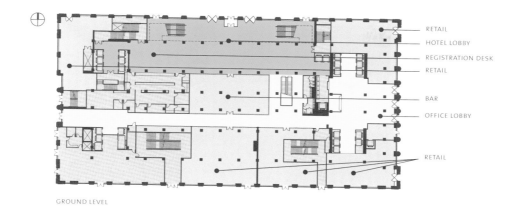

GROUND LEVEL

RETAIL
HOTEL LOBBY
REGISTRATION DESK
RETAIL

BAR
OFFICE LOBBY

RETAIL

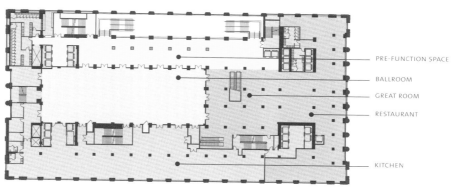

LEVEL 2

PRE-FUNCTION SPACE

BALLROOM
GREAT ROOM
RESTAURANT

KITCHEN

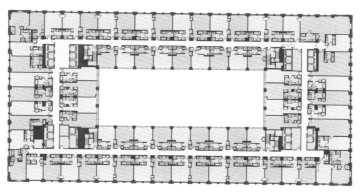

TYPICAL HOTEL PLAN, LEVEL 9

Previous page: The hotel lobby will include a new grand staircase. Top: The renovation creates separate entrances and lobbies for the hotel and office components while maintaining a significant amount of ground-floor retail space. Middle: The second floor—formerly a banking hall—is transformed into a restaurant and ballroom with kitchen space occupying the southwest corner. Bottom: Hotel rooms average 450 square feet.

SERVICE   LOBBY   CIRCULATION   RETAIL   AMENITIES   CONDO/HOTEL   CONFERENCE/BALLROOM

SLEEPY HOLLOW

7400 North Shore Drive
South Haven, Michigan
Year Completed: 2005

They are one of the more unexpected sights in Harbor Country, a Hamptons-like resort community near Chicago: 15 gleaming white Art Moderne structures—a mix of single and double cottages as well as one multi-unit apartment building—scattered around a 12-acre site fronting on Lake Michigan. The structures—along with a number of secondary buildings—are part of an unusual summer enclave established in the late 1930s by Edward Gray, a prominent Chicago industrialist. Art Moderne, the final incarnation of Art Deco, arrived in Chicago via the 1933 Century of Progress Exposition, which ran for two years on the city's lakefront. Mr. Gray, an admirer of the Exposition, requested a similar look for his project. The Gray family controlled the property until the late 1970s, at which point it became a condominium. By the late 1990s, however, the original wooden cottages had deteriorated beyond the point of repair. Lagrange was hired to propose alternatives. His solution involved replacing the existing cottages with new, slightly larger units that retained key features of the original's distinctive Art Moderne styling. The new cottages have wood frames along with cementitious siding that simulates stucco, a traditional Art Moderne building material. They also have full basements. Among the Art Moderne features are rounded bays, porthole windows, tubular balustrades and flat roofs. They range in size from 1,000 to 1,700 square feet and harmonize well with the remaining original buildings. Inside, the layouts are open and spacious and geared to views of the lake and park-like site. Lagrange also adjusted the site plan by re-routing several roads and upgrading the landscaping and parking areas.

 SITE PLAN

The new cottages are located along the northern periphery of the 12-acre site and within easy walking distance of the recreational facilities.

SITE   RESIDENCE   EXISTING STRUCTURES

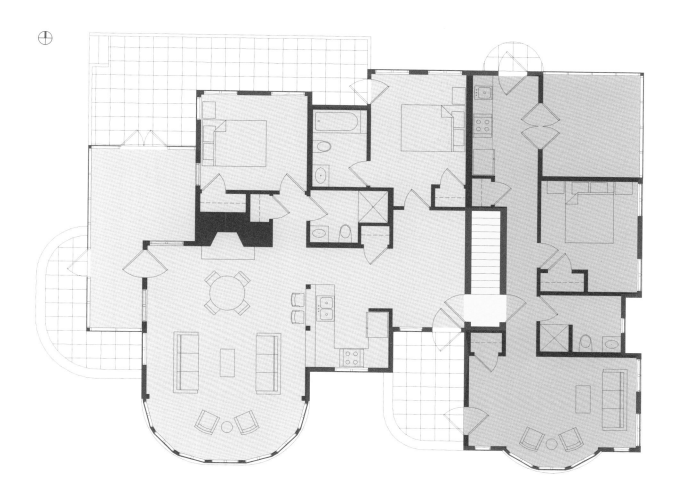

A typical cottage has both one- and two-bedroom units. Privacy is maintained by separating entryways and porches. Large bay windows provide views of the landscaped grounds.

 CIRCULATION RESIDENCE

LINCOLN PARK 2520

2550 Lakeview Avenue
Chicago, Illinois
Scheduled Completion Date: 2010

Lincoln Park is a compelling example of Lagrange's belief that style is often determined by market forces. The project started out as a Second Empire confection, then became Modern and eventually returned to a modified version of the original design. Throughout the process, the form and massing of the proposed building remained consistent. The ultimate deciding factors were neighborhood approval and the developer's feeling that buyers on this leafy street across from Lincoln Park would be more likely to embrace traditional rather than contemporary styling. That said, the building fits in well in a neighborhood that includes a number of the city's grandest pre-war apartment buildings. It's a huge project—306 apartments in the main structure, 12 townhouses and a one-acre private park. In addition, a landmark chapel left over from the hospital that formerly occupied the site had to be preserved and made accessible to the general public. Although one building in terms of interior systems and organization, Lagrange mitigates the monolithic nature of the project by breaking up the façade in a way that suggests three different buildings of varying heights.

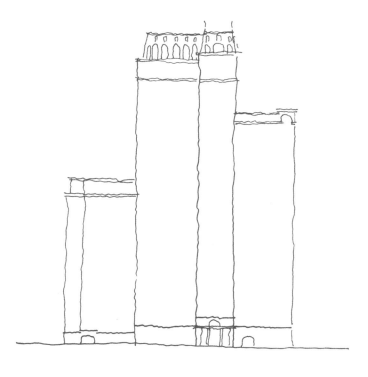

Above and next page: While the massing remained consistent, early studies for Lincoln Park 2520 explored both traditional and modern solutions.

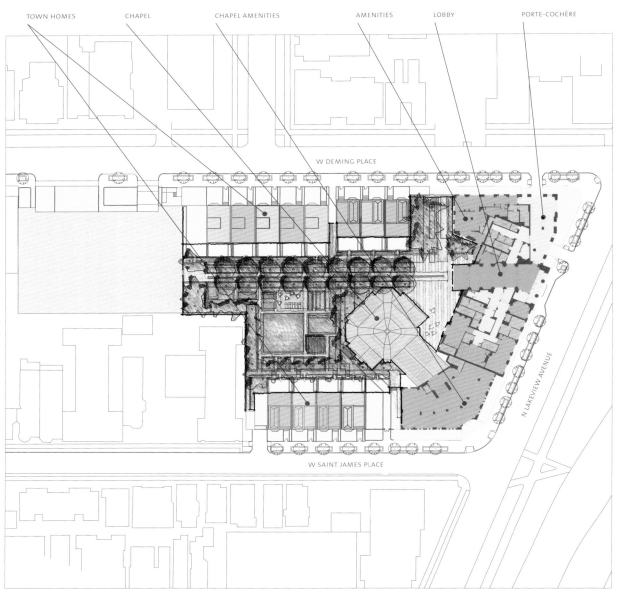

TOWN HOMES   CHAPEL   CHAPEL AMENITIES   AMENITIES   LOBBY   PORTE-COCHÈRE

W DEMING PLACE

N LAKEVIEW AVENUE

W SAINT JAMES PLACE

GROUND LEVEL AND SITE PLAN

Lincoln Park 2520's complex program involves a 37-story condominium building across from Lincoln Park, 12 town houses, and parking. At the center of the project is a landscaped one-acre garden. The project also includes an existing landmark chapel from the hospital that originally occupied the site. The chapel is publicly accessible through an entrance at the southeast corner.

SITE   SERVICE   LOBBY   CIRCULATION   PARKING   AMENITIES   CONDO/HOTEL

LEVELS 5–10

LEVELS 22–29

LEVEL 34

Top left: Two sets of elevators service the lower floors of the building, most of which are made up of one- and two-bedroom units. By including several floor-through units, a feeling of intimacy is created on the floor. Top right: The apartments grow larger as the building rises and include units with more than one exposure. Bottom: At the top are two 4,000-square-foot-plus penthouses, each with three balconies.

BELLE MAISON

60 West Erie Street
Chicago, Illinois
Year Completed: 2003

Belle Maison is one of Lagrange's more unusual buildings, an intimately
scaled mid-block condominium tower two blocks west of Michigan Avenue
that combines metal and masonry—and also color—in ways that recall
architect Auguste Perret's Art Nouveau inspired residential buildings in Belle
Epoch Paris. The site is tiny—barely 8,000 square feet, which is smaller than
some of the individual apartments in Lagrange's larger commissions. The
structure consists of a three-story base topped by a 17-story tower. The base is
buff-colored pre-cast stone, the upper floors painted concrete. Despite budget
constraints, there is a surprising amount of street-level detail in the form of
aluminum grills and stonework reveals. The defining feature is a teal blue
aluminum bay window that extends up the center of the façade. Balconies
on either side of the bay complete the latter's graceful curve. At the summit
is a delicate metal canopy that shades the terrace of the top-floor penthouse
and also serves as the building's pinnacle. The canopy is in the nature of an
architectural folie, a flourish that both completes the building and balances
the ornamentation at the base. The building has 24 apartments that range
in size from about 1,100 square feet up to about 3,700 square feet plus a
54-space parking garage.

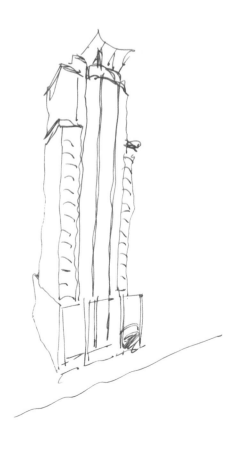

SERVICE SPACE

ELEVATOR LOBBY

LOADING DOCK

LOBBY

GROUND LEVEL

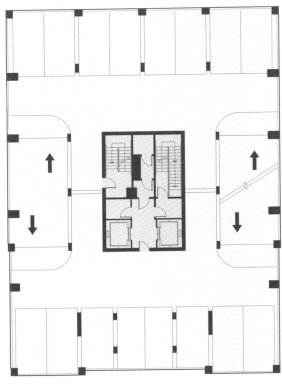

PARKING LEVEL

Top: Belle Maison's 8,000-square-foot ground floor includes a lobby, parking entrance, and extensive service areas. Bottom: Parking occupies floors two through five.

| SERVICE | LOBBY | CIRCULATION | PARKING | CONDO/HOTEL | PENTHOUSE |

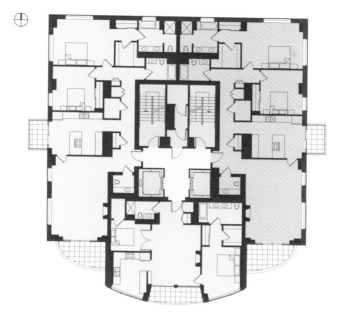

LEVELS 6–10, TYPICAL RESIDENTIAL PLAN

LEVELS 14–17, TYPICAL PENTHOUSE PLAN

Top: A typical floor has three two-bedroom units, all with large balconies. Bottom: The 3,000-square-foot top floor penthouse has four bedrooms.

PROJECT RAINBOW

Dublin, Ireland

This project—a proposal for a mixed-use, multi-building development on an irregular 7-acre site in downtown Dublin—gave Lagrange the opportunity to exercise the large-scale planning skills he honed in the early years of his career but which have played a relatively minor role in his Chicago work. At the heart of the project are two parallel thoroughfares—one for pedestrians, one for vehicular traffic—that curve through the development. The former is a covered retail arcade modeled after such historic shopping districts as London's Regent Street and Milan's Galleria. The arcade culminates in what amounts to a public square at the west end of the project. The vehicular street allows access to the office and residential components and also to an underground parking facility. Total square footage is 1.9 million square feet, which breaks down to 921,000 square feet of residential space, 412,000 square feet of retail space, 333,000 square feet of office space and 116,000 square feet of hotel space.

The different components are intermingled in a way that suggests the variety and vibrancy of a traditional city center. The project is surrounded on three sides primarily by two- and three-story residential buildings while the fourth side backs up against a commercial area. The massing takes this into account by locating the development's tallest buildings—three 32-story residential towers—near the commercial area. The project also preserves a row of historic trees along the perimeter of the site.

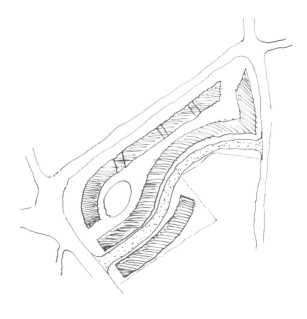

 GROUND LEVEL AND SITE PLAN

Project Rainbow's 7-acre site includes retail, office, and condominium buildings. Two roadways curve through the project — one for pedestrians that culminates in a town square and one for vehicular traffic. Mid-rise office and retail buildings line exterior streets and preserve the low- and mid-rise nature of the neighborhood. The project also preserves a row of historic trees along the periphery of the site.

SITE   RETAIL

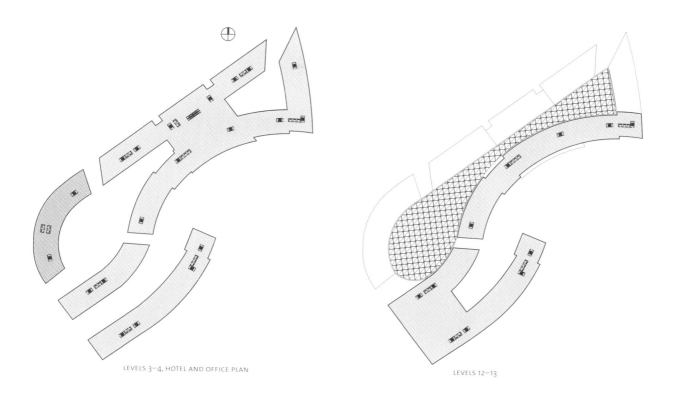

LEVELS 3–4, HOTEL AND OFFICE PLAN

LEVELS 12–13

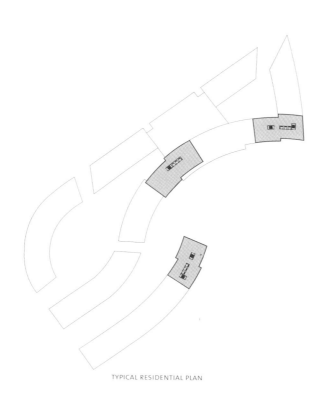

TYPICAL RESIDENTIAL PLAN

Top left: The project's lower levels are occupied by office and hotel space. Top right: Middle floors are a mix of office and residential condominium units. Note the glass canopy over the pedestrian walkway. Bottom: Three 32-story residential towers are located at the rear of the site.

SERVICE　　　LOBBY　　　CIRCULATION　　　PARKING　　　CONDO/HOTEL　　　PENTHOUSE

MANNHEIMER-LAGRANGE RESIDENCE

Chicago, Illinois
Year Completed: 1995

In 1884, when he designed this house for Leon Mannheimer, an accountant, Louis Sullivan was 28 years old and had only recently teamed up with Dankmar Adler in the firm of Adler & Sullivan. The firm had a lively residential practice in its early years and the Mannheimer house is one of about 40 residential commissions Sullivan executed during this period. Today, only a handful are left. The Mannheimer house is not a mansion. The scale throughout is relatively modest. The most interesting architectural feature is the first-floor bay window, a sharply protruding ship's prow that — in its bold geometry — recalls the work of Sullivan's early employer, Philadelphia architect Frank Furness. The house has gone through some rough periods — including a stint as a convalescent home in the 1950s — and when Lagrange acquired it in the early 1990s as his personal residence, it was in need of restoration. Numerous original details both inside and outside were either missing or had deteriorated beyond repair and had to be recreated. In a number of instances, educated guesses had to be made about Sullivan's intentions. For example, no photos or records of the original front doors or the living room fireplace mantle could be found. In both cases, Lagrange modeled the replacements on details from nearby Sullivan-designed residences from the same period. The great remaining interior feature — the front staircase with its remarkable balustrade — was cleaned and varnished. In the backyard, Lagrange designed an elegant garden with a fountain that delineates different spaces for dining and relaxing.

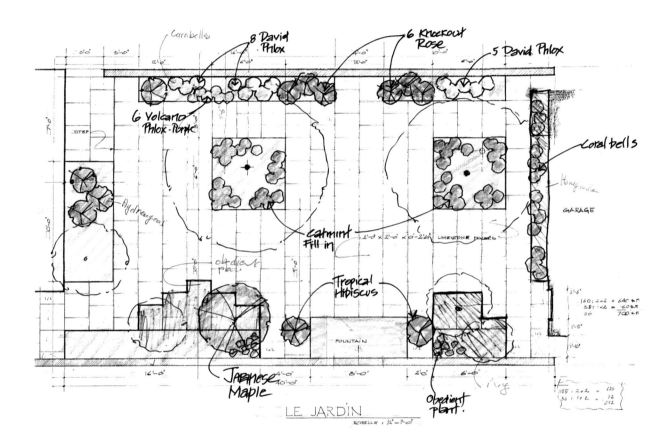

By relegating plantings mainly to the perimeter of the site, space is created for relaxing and entertaining.

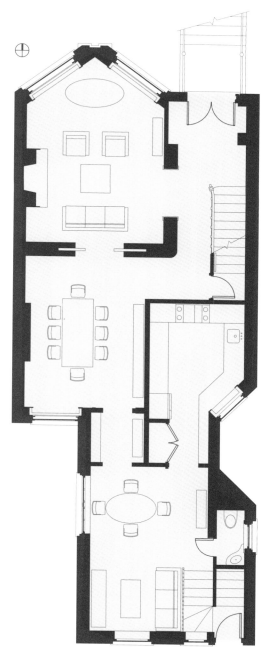

GROUND LEVEL

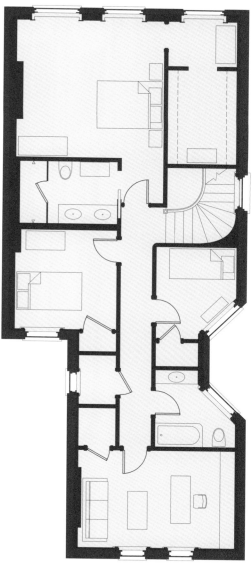

LEVEL 2

Left: Over the house's 123-year history, the original layout had been altered to the point where it was impossible to determine the location of the original kitchen. The front of the house is basically the way Sullivan designed it. The rest has been sensitively renovated to accommodate the demands of modern family life. Right: The second floor includes a new master suite, two additional bedrooms and a media room at the back of the house.

 CONDO

THE PINNACLE

21 East Huron Street
Chicago, Illinois
Year Completed: 2004

Climate and context were the uppermost considerations at The Pinnacle, a
35-story condominium tower in River North, a rapidly gentrifying district just
north of the Chicago River. The building—like most of the new condominium
buildings downtown—is constructed of reinforced concrete. Because concrete
weathers poorly in Chicago's harsh climate, however, the decision was made
to conceal most of the structure behind a beveled glass curtain wall. The
Pinnacle's graceful setbacks and Neo Gothic detailing are a nod to its neighbor
across the street, St. James Episcopal Cathedral. The Cathedral dates from 1857
and is considered one of the city's most important Gothic Revival structures.
The Pinnacle's setbacks also create a number of interesting terraces for the
upper-floor penthouses. The building has a four-story masonry base that
contains street level retail and parking. The beautifully rendered carved stone
display windows demonstrates Lagrange's belief in the importance of street
level detail and ornamentation.

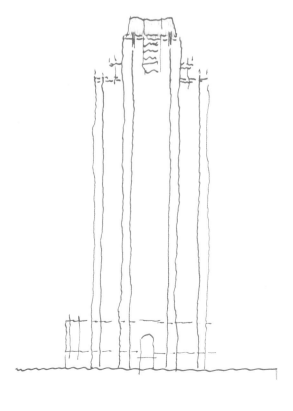

PARKING RAMP

RETAIL

LOBBY

LOADING DOCK

RETAIL

GROUND LEVEL

The Pinnacle's first floor contains the residential lobby and 10,312 square feet of retail space.

SERVICE   LOBBY   CIRCULATION   PARKING   RETAIL   CONDO/HOTEL   PENTHOUSE

LEVELS 16–26, TYPICAL RESIDENTIAL PLAN

LEVEL 48, PENTHOUSE PLAN

Left: A typical floor contains six apartments, all with one or more balconies. Right: At the top of the building are six penthouses that range in size from 5,400 square feet to 8,000 square feet.

FIFTY-FIVE WEST MONROE LOBBY

55 West Monroe Street
Chicago, Illinois
Year Completed: 2001

The first-floor circulation pattern of this 1980s office building needed to be adjusted to reflect recent security concerns. In addition, the building was experiencing occupancy problems and a new, more contemporary lobby played a key role in the owner's marketing plans. The former objective was accomplished by re-directing all traffic past a central reception desk. The latter involved installing a new terrazzo floor as well as new lighting that provided a softer, more appealing illumination. In addition, curved cherry wood panels soften the contours of the original design and add a touch of warmth and color to the space.

PROJECT X

Chicago Illinois

Planned for an 8,000-square-foot site in Chicago's Loop commercial district, this 71-story glass prism of a building is a celebration of structure. The eight reinforced concrete super columns—two on each side—are locked in place by a series of diagonal braces on every third floor. There are no interior columns. In addition, a tuned mass damper system at the summit minimizes building sway. Stairs, elevators, and utilities are contained in a core that rises up through the center of the building. The tower has 388 apartments that range in size from 800 square feet to 2,250 square feet, all of which have either balconies or terraces.

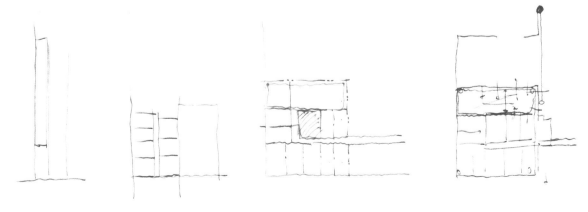

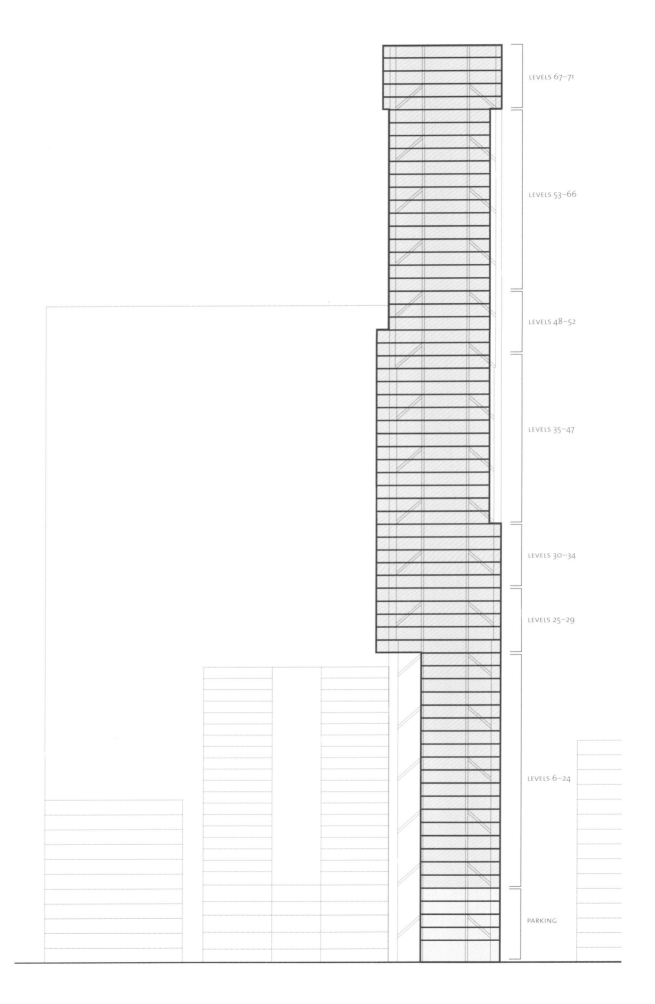

LEVELS 67–71

LEVELS 53–66

LEVELS 48–52

LEVELS 35–47

LEVELS 30–34

LEVELS 25–29

LEVELS 6–24

PARKING

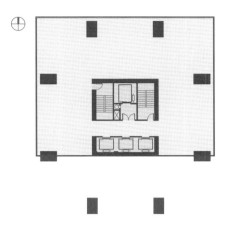

LEVELS 6–24

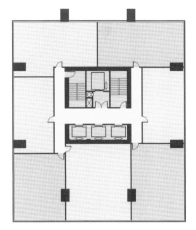

LEVELS 35–47

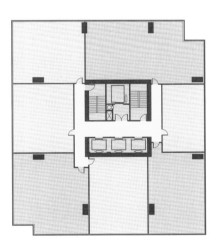

LEVELS 53–66

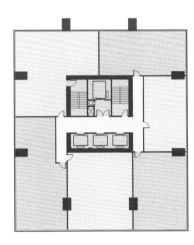

LEVELS 67–71

Previous page: By alternately exposing and concealing the structural piers, the building—basically a glass box—creates a striking silhouette on the skyline.
Above: The building has 388 apartments that range in size from 800 square feet to 2,250 square feet.

 SERVICE   CIRCULATION   PARKING   CONDO/HOTEL

WEST END RESIDENCES

531–39 West End Avenue
New York, New York
Scheduled Completion Date: 2009

Lagrange's first New York project — a 20-story condominium building — anchors a busy corner on the Upper West Side, a neighborhood composed largely of vintage brownstones and pre-war apartment blocks. The area is ultra genteel and — in its sophisticated mix of uses and proximity to Central Park — not that different from similar neighborhoods in Lagrange's beloved Paris. West End blends into this environment in an effortless way. There is genuine restraint and civility in the way the building's setback both acknowledges its neighbors and sets the stage for the upper floor penthouses. City living is about choices. West End's 15th-floor unit with its enormous wrap-around terrace is a choice many city dwellers would like to make.

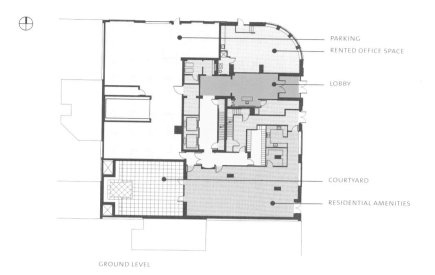

GROUND LEVEL

PARKING
RENTED OFFICE SPACE
LOBBY
COURTYARD
RESIDENTIAL AMENITIES

LEVELS 8–13, TYPICAL RESIDENTIAL PLAN

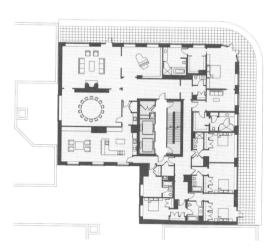

LEVEL 15, TYPICAL RESIDENTIAL PLAN WITH FULL TERRACE

Top: In addition to the lobby, the ground floor has 1,600 square feet of rentable office space. Middle: The 20-story building contains 11 full-floor apartments that range in size from 6,313 square feet to 8,132 square feet. To ensure privacy, the bedrooms are sequestered away from the living and entertaining spaces. The curved corner room invites a number of different uses. Bottom: The 15th-floor unit includes a wrap-around terrace.

SERVICE   LOBBY   CIRCULATION   PARKING   OFFICE   AMENITIES   CONDO/HOTEL

THE RITZ-CARLTON RESIDENCES

664 North Michigan Avenue
Chicago, Illinois
Scheduled Completion Date: 2009

The Ritz Carlton Residences is Lagrange's second condominium project on Michigan Avenue, Chicago's equivalent of Fifth Avenue in New York or the Champs-Élysées in Paris. The first, Park Tower, was completed in 2000. Like Park Tower, the Ritz acknowledges its high-profile site by including street-level retail and by incorporating a landmark building—in this case, the 10-story Farwell Building—into its program. Stylistically, both Park Tower and the Ritz take their cues from the area's history as a premier commercial district in the 1920s, a period that saw the construction of a number of graceful Art Deco commercial buildings by architects such as Philip Maher and Thielbar & Fugard. The Ritz rises 40 stories on an irregular 12,000-square-foot site with an asymmetrical stepped pinnacle topped by an illuminated crown. The building contains 86 condominiums, including two penthouses. There are also 167 parking spaces and 8,000 square feet of retail space on the ground level.

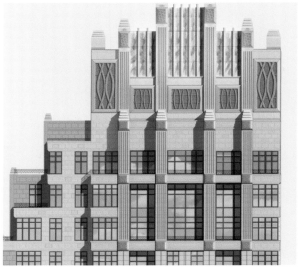

Left: The Ritz incorporates architect Philip Maher's 1927 Farwell Building at the corner of Michigan Avenue and Erie Street. Right: The building's asymmetrical pinnacle includes an illuminated crown.

The 10th-floor lounge includes space for socializing and entertaining.

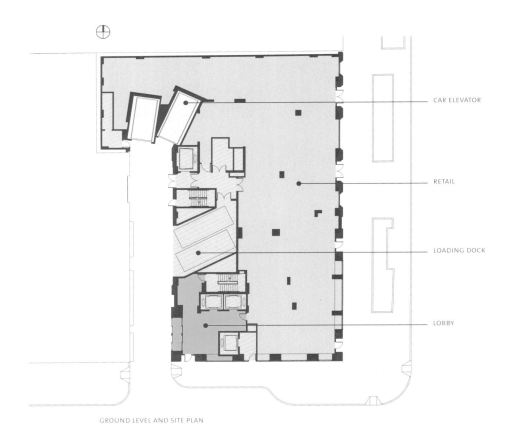

CAR ELEVATOR

RETAIL

LOADING DOCK

LOBBY

GROUND LEVEL AND SITE PLAN

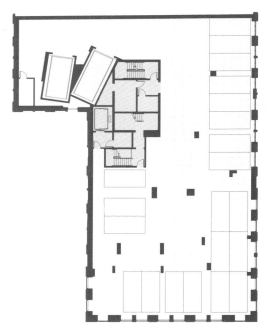

LEVELS 2–9, PARKING

Top: The Ritz has a Michigan Avenue address but the residential lobby is around the corner on Erie Street. The ground floor contains 8,000 square feet of retail space. Bottom: The building's lower floors are occupied by parking and building services space.

SERVICE	LOBBY	CIRCULATION	PARKING	OFFICE	RETAIL	AMENITIES
CONDO/HOTEL	CONFERENCE/BALLROOM					

PARKING

CAR ELEVATOR

OFFICE SPACE

LEVELS 3–5, PARKING AND OFFICE SPACE

SAUNA

SPA

ELEVATOR LOBBY

FITNESS ROOM

KITCHEN

BILLIARDS AND
WINE ROOM

MEDIA ROOM

RECEPTION

ELEVATOR LOBBY

BOARD ROOM

GREAT ROOM

LEVEL 10, CLUB FLOOR

LEVELS 15–21, TYPICAL 4-UNIT RESIDENTIAL PLAN

LEVEL 40, PENTHOUSE PLAN

Top left: The base of the building contains 167 parking spaces and 12,324 square feet of office space. Top right: The 10th floor includes a spa and fitness area as well as social spaces. Bottom left: The Ritz's interior layouts are unusually varied and interesting due to the notched footprint of the tower. Bottom right: The 6,050-square-foot penthouse has unobstructed views in all directions.

CHICAGO UNION STATION

210 South Canal Street
Chicago, Illinois
Scheduled Completion Date: 2010

During the first half of the 20th century, railroad stations played a leading role in the social and economic life of most American cities. Architect Daniel Burnham acknowledged this reality in his 1909 Plan of Chicago by giving what ultimately became Union Station a prominent location halfway between Lake Michigan and what he envisioned would be a new civic center half a mile west of downtown. The center never materialized but the station—ultimately built just east of Burnham's suggested site—has been an instant landmark since the day it opened in 1925. Burnham died in 1912 and the commission passed to his successor firm, Graham, Anderson, Probst & White. Graham, Anderson's design consisted of two buildings: a headhouse with an enormous main waiting room as well as spaces for stores, restaurants and ticketing facilities plus a concourse across the street where passengers actually boarded or departed the dozens of trains that passed through the station on a daily basis. The two buildings were connected by an underground passageway. The original plan called for the headhouse to be topped by a 20-story office tower. This was eventually downsized to three additional floors that are more or less invisible from the street. Train travel declined precipitously after World War II and the concourse building was demolished in 1969 and replaced by a fairly dismal modern office tower that retains the boarding platforms as well as the underground passageway in one of its sub-basements. Lagrange first became involved with Union Station in 1985 when Amtrak, the owner of the terminal, hired him to undertake a renovation for the purpose of smoothing out traffic patterns for the station's commuter passengers and constructing a new ticketing and waiting area adjacent to the boarding platforms. Both projects essentially routed people away from the magnificent but significantly underutilized headhouse. Since then, there have been three attempts—two and a half, really, since the third is basically a slight reconfiguring of the second—to expand and revitalize the station. All have involved Lagrange. The first, which died with the collapse of the real estate market in the early 1990s, called for a twin tower addition to the headhouse. The second, 10 years later, involved extending the building along the lines originally proposed by Graham Anderson but with a modern interior consisting of offices, a hotel, and residential condominiums grouped around a soaring atrium featuring the distinctive diagonal bracing Lagrange has made his trademark and topped by an elaborate glass skylight. The third and current version rejiggers several of these elements—more offices, fewer condos—but preserves the essential vision. Meanwhile, the spectacular main waiting room as well as the now unused commercial spaces will be restored and will serve as both a lobby for the floors above and an enclosed public square for the surrounding neighborhood.

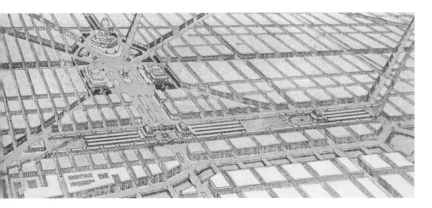

Top left: A rendering of the 1909 Burnham plan showing Union Station just west of the Chicago River. Top right: The original station was designed by Graham, Anderson, Probst and White and consisted of two buildings, the headhouse or waiting room and the now demolished concourse fronting on the river. Bottom: The station as it appears today.

Lagrange's plan for renovating and expanding the station calls for adding another 18 floors. The Neo-Classical façade is based on an unbuilt addition by the original architects.

Above: One of two entrances for the office component. Next page: The office lobbies are on the mezzanine level and look out over the restored main waiting room.

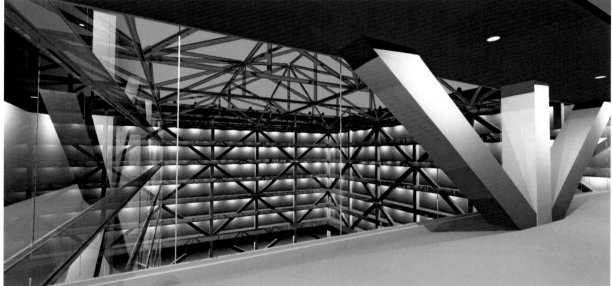

The interior atrium with its diagonal bracing culminates in a glass skylight.

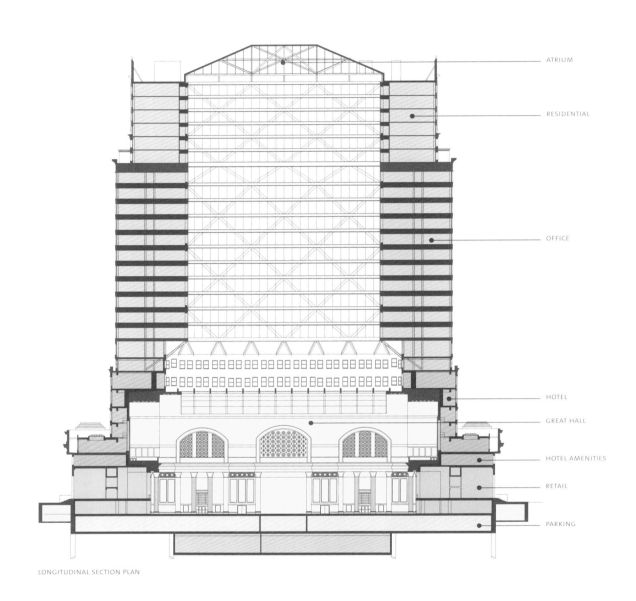

ATRIUM

RESIDENTIAL

OFFICE

HOTEL

GREAT HALL

HOTEL AMENITIES

RETAIL

PARKING

LONGITUDINAL SECTION PLAN

The reconfigured terminal will include 180 condominiums, 613,000 square feet of office space, 322 hotel rooms, and 90,000 square feet of retail space.

SERVICE   LOBBY   CIRCULATION   OFFICE   RETAIL   AMENITIES   CONDO/HOTEL

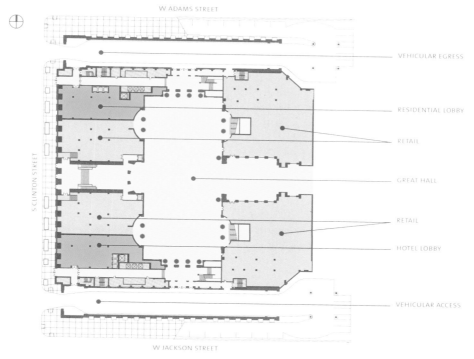

W ADAMS STREET

VEHICULAR EGRESS

RESIDENTIAL LOBBY

RETAIL

S CLINTON STREET

GREAT HALL

RETAIL

HOTEL LOBBY

VEHICULAR ACCESS

W JACKSON STREET

CLINTON GROUND LEVEL AND SITE PLAN

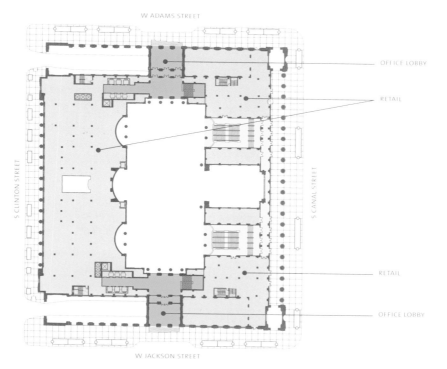

W ADAMS STREET

OFFICE LOBBY

RETAIL

S CLINTON STREET

S CANAL STREET

RETAIL

OFFICE LOBBY

W JACKSON STREET

CANAL GROUND LEVEL AND SITE PLAN

Top: The first level will have a substantial amount of retail space in addition to separate lobbies for the residential and hotel components.
Bottom: The mezzanine level includes duo lobbies for the office component and additional retail space.

A CONVERSATION WITH LUCIEN LAGRANGE
Robert Sharoff and Lucien Lagrange

Top: Robert Sharoff and Lucien Lagrange. Bottom: Lagrange's mother, Flora, raking hay in Monthlery in the 1940s. In the background is the surprisingly modern flat-roofed house designed and built by Lagrange's father, Lucien Sr.

RS: I know you grew up in France, but what was your family like?

LL: We weren't aristocrats. My father had to go to work at age nine. His father died and he had to leave school and go work on a farm. The same thing happened to my mother. Her father died when she was 11. He was kicked in the chest by a horse.

RS: It sounds primitive.

LL: It was. Right up until World War II, France—at least in the countryside, which is where I mainly grew up—was like living in the Middle Ages. Not that much had changed. Then the war came and everything got worse. There was very little food in those years. Everybody was hungry. The only way we survived was that my mother had grown up on a farm and knew how to raise rabbits and chickens and grow potatoes and cabbages and tomatoes. It was a very different time and place. But it's where I come from.

RS: How does that affect the way you look at the world?

LL: I've never taken anything for granted. When I was in college at McGill, a lot of the students came from well off families. They felt entitled to a degree and a successful career. I never felt entitled to anything. I always felt on edge—am I going to pass? Am I going to fail? Failure always seemed possible.

RS: Do you think you could have had the same career if you had stayed in France?

LL: No. No way. Even today, France is very divided by class. It's a closed world. You've got to come from the right family, the right school and have the right connections in order to get ahead. I didn't have any of that. I was a high school drop out.

Peter Collins, Norbert Schoenauer and Bruce Graham.

RS: Who do you feel has had the most influence on your career?

LL: The three men who influenced me the most were Peter Collins, Norbert Schoenauer and Bruce Graham. The first two were professors of mine at McGill and Bruce, of course, is Bruce. Collins taught me about architectural process and where ideas come from. Schoenauer opened my eyes to housing and how all architecture—not just residential—is about people and lifestyles before it's about anything else.

RS: In 1968, you began your association with Skidmore, Owings & Merrill. What was your initial impression of the firm?

LL: It was an outstanding place to learn the process of architecture because they had projects, big projects. They were great at putting buildings together, which is what I still do. Before you worry about aesthetics, a building has to stand up, it has to be put together. At Skidmore, I learned how to do that.

RS: Skidmore was Modernist to the core. How did you fit into that environment?

LL: I never made much of an intellectual connection at Skidmore. In fact, it was kind of oppressive, mainly because it was only about one thing and that was Mies. But, at least in the beginning, they did some amazing work. When I arrived, Bruce was designing the Hancock Building, which is probably the last Chicago building to have a global impact on architecture. It's gutsy. It's the pure expression of what a building should be.

Left: Bruce Graham's John Hancock Centre on Michigan Avenue in downtown Chicago. "The last Chicago building to have a global impact on architecture." Right: Lagrange's Onterie Center in Chicago.

RS: What are your favorite projects from that period?

LL: The three I'm proudest of are Dearborn Park, Onterie Center, and One Financial Place. All are in Chicago. Dearborn Park is a residential building, Onterie Center is residential and offices and One Financial is a little bit of everything except residential—offices, a hotel, retail, a health club with an Olympic-size swimming pool and a train station. Those are the buildings where I really started to break away from the traditional Skidmore box and try for something that felt more alive.

RS: You were very much associated with Bruce Graham in those years. How did the two of you get along?

LL: Bruce liked me. Partly, I think, because I could take a dead project and bring it back to life. I could look at a plan that wasn't working and see why and suggest a new direction. I got something very important from Bruce. I remember flying out with him once to do a presentation for the CEO of a big company and I was nervous and embarrassed because back then my accent was even worse than it is today. He said a wonderful thing: "Don't worry. You've got your own style. Just do it." He was right. Just be honest. Don't try to be something you're not. It's how I still operate today.

RS: In 1985, you left to form your own firm. What was that experience like?

LL: I moved six drafting tables into an office at One Financial Place and started calling people up looking for work. It felt like I had been thrown into the deep end of a swimming pool without a life preserver. I went from designing huge highrises and complicated multi-use projects to drafting tenant improvements for 25 cents per square foot. But I never regretted it. I slept much better after I left Skidmore. I also learned something that meant a great deal to me.

RS: What's that?

LL: That I actually had a lot of friends. After I left, so many people told me they respected my decision to go out on my own and offered to help in any way they could. It made a big difference. I didn't feel so alone even though I pretty much was back in the early days.

RS: Your style changed dramatically at that point. What happened?

LL: I'm not sure anything happened. At Skidmore, I designed Skidmore buildings. It was my job. But it was never my style. I don't know if I have a style. I have a method and there are certain principles in which I believe. But it's not really a style. My work has a lot to do with precedent, which is something Modern architects are never supposed to admit. You're supposed to maintain this fantasy that architecture began in the 20th century and everything that came before is completely irrelevant. But that's impossible. Ideas have to come from somewhere and the past is often a good place to start.

Details of various Parisian apartment buildings photographed by Lagrange.

RS: You are obviously very drawn to Classicism.

LL: I am. There are apartment buildings in Paris I go and look at over and over again. I think they're beautiful. But I am also fascinated by Chicago. I love those wonderful old buildings from the 1920s in the Loop and along Lake Shore Drive.

RS: What do you admire about those earlier styles?

LL: The liveliness, the humanity. The fact that they all have a base, a shaft and a top in addition to a well articulated entrance. I'm a firm believer that the base of a building needs to be richer in detail than the rest because people can see and touch it. These are all pretty basic architectural principles but they're also things that somehow went out of style in the 1960s and 70s. I mean, take a good look at the Sears Tower. There's no top and no bottom. It's all middle. I always found that kind of disturbing.

RS: You are sometimes criticized for your eclecticism. People seem to think that architects should stick to one look or style. How do you respond to that?

LL: Well, I don't respond. But I don't understand it. Why should designers limit themselves like that? Do you know the story of the original Les Halles market in Paris?

RS: No.

LL: Back in 1853, Napoleon III decided Paris needed a new central market. He asked Baron Haussmann to find an architect to design one. Haussmann suggested Victor Baltard, a good friend of his. Baltard designed this beautiful building with heavy stone arches—the kind of thing you would normally do back then for a conservative client. Haussmann took the drawings to Napoleon III, who said, "It's not what I want at all. I want something very high tech and modern. Fire this guy and find somebody else." So Haussmann went back to Baltard and said you need to change your design because the emperor wants something very high tech. So Baltard did. He came up with those beautiful metal sheds everyone still remembers. The point is that a designer designs. Why the Modernists thought a glass box was the answer to everything I'll never understand.

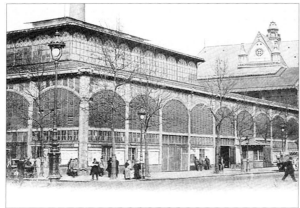

Victor Baltard's now-demolished Les Halles market in Paris.

RS: The project that established you as an independent architect was Park Tower, a 68- story hotel and condominium tower on Water Tower Square in Chicago that is one of the tallest buildings in the world. How did it come about?

Park Tower in Chicago, Lagrange's largest commission to date.

LL: Park Tower had a long gestation period. It originally was going to be located where Plaza Escada is today on Michigan Avenue but the deal never came together. A few years later, however, the developers decided to try again at a different site a block south that fronts on Water Tower Square. When I think about it, the delay actually was a blessing in disguise because the new site is far more exciting.

RS: What's special about it?

LL: It's basically at the head of this tremendous urban lawn that rolls on for four or five blocks and ends at Lake Michigan. It's kind of astounding.

RS: Why did you decide to do an Art Deco-inspired building?

LL: Many reasons. It goes with the street. Michigan Avenue at one time was known for its Art Deco buildings. But it's also a function of the site—which is fairly small—and the fact that it's a very tall building. That limits your options.

RS: Is it one of your favorites?

LL: I get a lot of compliments on that building. It's also one of the most financially successful buildings of my career and, believe me, that's not nothing. But at the same time, I lost some battles during construction that continue to bug me. For instance, I wanted the windows to be recessed seven inches and they got value engineered back to four inches.

RS: What got lost?

LL: The shadows. It's a subtle thing. Deep windows give a building weight and definition. And with a stone building, that's important. All that aside, however, it's still pretty strong. There are some basic strengths there—like the slenderness of the tower and the interior layouts—that you can't ignore. In a way, the building is like a beautiful woman—even if you don't like the dress she's wearing, she's still beautiful.

RS: In recent years, the building of yours that has received the most attention is Erie on the Park, a Modern building. Were you surprised by the reception it received?

LL: It's one of those projects that came along at exactly the right moment. The market changed, Modernism looked good again and Erie was the first building—at least in Chicago—to reflect that. I wish I could say I knew all that going in but, really, it had more to do with the neighborhood and site than anything else. It's an old industrial neighborhood and the site is close to impossible. You certainly would not do a classical or traditional building there. Also, there was a blip in steel prices at the end of the nineties and steel suddenly became feasible for a year or two.

RS: How do you start designing a building?

LL: At first, it's all about information—endless data about the site, the client, the program, the budget. But information by itself doesn't really tell you what a building should be. That's where your own talent and experience comes into play. Projects tend to happen in bursts. You think about them and think about them and then, suddenly, almost magically, it all comes together in your mind. Years ago, I remember Bruce Graham coming back from LA and calling me into his office one morning to discuss what became Citicorp Plaza. He laid it all out in five minutes: three towers, two department stores, 1,600 cars, a highway that had to be rerouted. It was like, Boom! He had it. Those are the moments you live for as an architect. The rest is just filling in the details.

RS: How do you know what's right style-wise for a given job?

LL: There's no formula. It emerges out of the program. For instance, I'm designing a residential building on Michigan Avenue right now for Ritz Carlton, which, of course, is a very old, very established luxury brand name. The units are priced at $1,000 per square foot, which is top of the market in Chicago. All of this—the location, the name and the price level—tells me that the people who are going to live there are going to be conservative. Also, there's a landmark 1920s building on the site that has to be preserved. When you combine these factors, you arrive at the conclusion that a traditional stone building is probably the best solution.

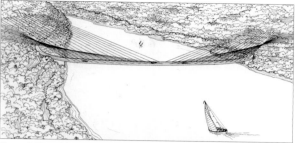

Myron Goldsmith's Ruck-A-Chucky Bridge. "People call it the most beautiful bridge never built."

RS: What role does aesthetics play in your thinking?

LL: When I was in school, one of my math teachers spent an entire day writing out the calculations for a very complicated problem on the blackboard. In the end, he got the whole thing down to a simple equation. I remember him saying, "I think this is beautiful." Architecture is like that. There is always an element of searching. You start with the constants of the program and you search for the most elegant solution. Have you ever seen renderings of the bridge Myron Goldsmith designed back in the 70s? It's called Ruck-A-Chucky Bridge. People call it the most beautiful bridge never built. The concrete is so thin it becomes beautiful. It's an example of using materials in the most creative, elegant and efficient way. But it takes time.

RS: Are you ever surprised by buildings after they're up? Do they sometimes turn out better or worse than you thought they would?

LL: Very rarely. But at times they will have qualities I didn't anticipate. For example, friends of mine, a couple, live at 65 East Goethe. When I first walked into their apartment, I was struck by the fact that, because it's a U-shaped building, they get natural light from opposite directions. It's a very nice effect. I wasn't thinking about that when I designed it, however. At the time, I just thought a U-shaped footprint was the best way to capture square footage.

RS: Do you have projects where you wish you had walked away?

LL: Of course. Every architect has a few. What happens is you hang in with a project that's going in the wrong direction because you think you can save it or somehow make it work. I did a project out in the Chicago suburbs where the developer took on a new partner midway through and suddenly the whole program changed. What started out as a nice mid-rise development with condos and some retail grouped around a little plaza suddenly doubled in size. Everything—the scale, the planning—changed and not for the better. I knew it was wrong but I stayed anyway, thinking I could make it work. Big mistake. Because my name's on it and people still ask me why I did something so out of scale with the rest of the neighborhood. It's one of those lessons you learn.

RS: You've been quoted as saying you prefer the real estate world to the architecture world. What do you mean by that?

LL: I prefer the real estate world because it's a more real world. I think architecture for architecture's sake has made a lot of mistakes. When I first started my practice, one of the major parts of my business was renovating Modern buildings from the 1960s and 70s. Why? Because they weren't done right in the first place. The architects back then didn't give people the environment in which they wanted to live and work.

RS: That's a pretty sweeping indictment.

LL: I have strong feelings about it. Have you ever seen Le Corbusier's worker housing?

RS: In photographs.

Le Corbusier's worker housing project in Pessac, France, after alterations.

LL: It's all pretty similar: flat roofs, big bay windows, no ornament, God forbid. In Modern terms, it's beautiful. But if you go back and look at those projects now, however, they've all been altered. The residents have added pitched roofs, awnings and flower boxes. Because that's how they want to live. You can't just ignore that.

RS: You take a very active interest in the interiors of your buildings and in particular issues like floor plans and traffic patterns. Many architects turn these particulars over to associates. Why do you feel it's important to be involved in these matters?

LL: It goes back to my training with Norbert Schoenauer and his emphasis on lifestyle as a driving force in design. The floor plan is where all that is reflected. I'm doing a condominium building in New York right now and after researching the market and talking to people I've come to realize it's very different from Chicago. In New York, it's not unusual for families to spend all of their lives in apartments. But in Chicago, most couples buy a house after they have their first or second child.

RS: How does that affect design?

LL: In New York, it means you need a lot of bedrooms and they're grouped together so that the parents can hear the kids at night. But in Chicago, where the residents are singles and young couples and emptynesters, you have fewer bedrooms and you split them up. There's no reason to have all the bedrooms grouped around the master suite.

RS: How does that play out in other rooms?

LL: It depends. Lately, what I see happening with floor plans is that kitchens are getting smaller and smaller. The reason is people cook less and they don't have all the dishes and silver they used to so there's less need for cabinets and counter space. I see it in my own life. My wife and I have all of this family silver that comes out at Thanksgiving and Christmas. The rest of the year, it's in storage and we never use it.

RS: But you still have it.

LL: That's true. Actually, it's interesting how one day can affect the design of an apartment. A big dilemma for American architects when they're doing kitchens is figuring out how to accommodate Thanksgiving dinner. Even if the owners eat out for the rest of the year, on that one day you know they're going to have 20 people over for dinner. You have to design for that.

RS: One of your specialties is luxury apartments. After 20 years, what do you know about the rich?

LL: That they have more money than I do. Also, that they tend to be conservative, which I don't suppose comes as much of a surprise. But income by itself is only one piece of the puzzle. I'm doing an apartment right now for a very prominent client. It's big—5,000 square feet—but he's using it mainly as a pied-à-terre because he has three other houses. But he and his wife need space in the city to entertain and do fundraising for different causes. Once you understand that, you can give them what they need—a gallery instead of a corridor, a spectacular dining room, a kitchen geared to catering. This is about business, not family life.

RS: You have also developed a specialty in restoring and renovating historic buildings, often in dramatic ways. There seems to be a lot of controversy in the profession about how to deal with landmark structures. What is your philosophy?

LL: It is controversial. Basically, today, you cannot touch a landmark structure. It has to look exactly like it did in 1920 or whenever it was built. I don't necessarily agree with this approach but it's what we have to deal with in most cases.

RS: What is your objection?

LL: I remember a lecture Peter Collins once gave on Versailles at McGill. Versailles began as a small hunting lodge for one of the Bourbon kings. Then it got too small and they started adding wings. Nobody thought anything about it. Can you imagine trying to design a wing for Versailles today? You'd be crucified. And what exactly should be landmarked—the original hunting lodge? The lodge plus the first wing? It's a real dilemma for architects. But it is the world we're living in.

The hunting lodge that became Versailles. "Can you imagine trying to design a wing for Versailles today? You'd be crucified."

RS: How do you work within those limitations?

LL: I'm currently doing an addition for Union Station in Chicago, which was originally designed by Graham, Anderson, Probst & White in the teens and 20s. Union Station today is very underutilized. That huge waiting room everyone loves is barely used. But even so, getting an addition approved would normally be a very difficult process. Luckily for us, however, somewhere in there Graham, Anderson actually designed an addition that never got built and that's what we're building. It's going to be classical on the outside but with a modern interior. That's one way to solve it.

RS: Lucien Lagrange Associates recently celebrated its 20th anniversary. What do you see for the next 20 years?

LL: Several years ago, I reorganized the office and brought in some new project managers. The goal is to be large enough to do projects like Union Station but not so large that management takes over. I want to remain design-oriented. One of the things I really enjoy about what I do is that I get to be both large and small. In a typical day, I can have a meeting about a 70-story building and another about the stone floor of a certain apartment.

RS: Do you enter many competitions?

LL: Some. But I don't particularly like them. To me, they don't make sense because you're designing in a vacuum with little input from the client. I really believe there are many ways to do a given project and that the client needs to be in on the decision-making process. If you look at the great buildings of the world, there are always strong clients behind them.

RS: Do you see any one style predominating in the future?

LL: No. I don't want to limit myself that way.

RS: I know you recently went to Dubai to discuss doing a project there.

LL: It's not for me. It's so new—50 years ago they were all living in tents. There's no real urban context. So what do you do? You try to please the sheik, who has been looking at magazines. Everybody is trying to outdo their neighbor in terms of craziness or wildness. And when you look at the buildings, they're cartoons. Give me Chicago, where at least you have a continuum in terms of history and culture and society. It gives you a starting point. In architecture, ultimately, there has to be meaning. You don't do something just because it's fun or you like it. You're affecting the society you live in and it's going to last a hundred years. It's not disposable.

FIRM LISTING SINCE 1985
As of September 2007

Iffat Afsana
Kristi Ahlstrom
Xiaochun Ai
Angelica Alanis
Michael Allen
Stuart Allen
Benjamin Alvey
Nadia Anderson
Thomas Arends
Susan Augustine
Amanda Babcock
Forest Bahruth
Yelena Baybus
Mike Bazzell
Jolanta Beclawska
Diane Behn
Lisa Bell
Jessica Biondo
Dan Biver
Denis Blanc
Anita Bonilla
Matt Booma
Rachel Branagan
Wayne Brewer
Robert Brolin
Adrienne Brown
Don Brown
Brian Buczkowski
Jody Buell
Javier Burciaga
Severine Cahane
Steve Cannella
Irene Cardona
Christine Carter-Eggers
Philip Castillo
Veronica Castillo
Young Chai
John Christopher
Michael Clark
Joseph Cliggott
Brett Cochrane
Matthew Coglianese
Dan Csoka
Anita Csordas
Michael Dalezman
Rebecca Daly
Sean Daly
Jeffery Dalzell
Garrett Daniel
Melissa Danielson
Lisa Delaney
Jeffery Densic

Judy Deschamps
Randall Deutsch
Jackie Diesing
Alanna Dillman
Jason Dowling
Iliana Doytcheva
Jennifer Duffy
Marcel Eberle
Adam Emery
Kyle Fell
Dan Figatner
Amy Finley
William Foellmer
Deborah Fox
Whitney Fruin
Vivian Fung
Robert Gamperl
Laura Garcia
Jonathan Gibson
Joshua Gilbert
Renato Gilberti
Kristina Glusac
Jennifer Goodlove
Vallerie Gordon
Elizabeth Graffagna
Amy Graves
Tangi Griggs
Daniel Guich
Madhu Gupta
Bryce Hanna
Corrine Hara
Peter Harlan
Chadd Harrison
Charles Hasbrouck
Karen Hill
Timothy Hill
Robert Hillery
Laura Himel
Cayl Hollis
Jeanne Homer
Hideo Homma
Doreen Hsu
David Huggins
Yoo Joung Hwang
Christopher Ingrassia
Darryl Jackson
Theresa Johnson
Nick Juhasz
Kathia Kacic
Richard Kalb
Mike Karlovitz
Elicia Keebler Gibbon

James Kemper
Reynauldt Keys
Duk Ju Kim
Sung-Jung Kim
Jessica Kindred
Mark Kinn
Gary Kohn
Dianne Kontos
Victor Krasnopolsky
Pauline Kurtides
Kenneth Lacerda
Jessica Lagrange
Lucien Lagrange
My-Nga Lam
Manuel Lamboy
Orest Lang
Lindsey Lanzisero
Roxane LaStrapes
Chris Lee
Joong Lee
So Young Lee
Sung Ryong Lee
John Lenti
Michael Levin
Peter Leoschke
Patrick Libera
Julie Liska
Chris Loftus
Nicole Louviere
Kara Mann
Alfredo Marr
Enrique Martinez
Harry Martinez
Kavitha Marudadu
Michael Maurer
Cecilia McAgy
Murray McPhillips
Brian Meade
Oscar Medellin
Ray Meek
Nital Mehta
Carol Mergl
Dennis Milam
Casey Milbrand
Kristine Miller
Michael Miller
Rebecca Miller
Wayne Miller
Susan Mitchell
Kathryn Moon
Dean Mueller
Lisa Mueller

Tiffany Nash
Jeffrey Nelson
Sutaya Nesius
Deborah Norman
Chris Oakley
Darci Oberly
John Ostendorf
Eric Overby
Wojtek Palmowski
JB Park
Ryan Pavlik
Jessica Pearre
Kathryn Phillips
Natalie Phillips
Shawn Phillips
Stella Quinlan
Atefeh Rahimpour
Deborah Rashman
Susan Reid
Margarita Retana
Travis Rich
Ryan Rivard
Eric Robinson
Stephen Rogers
Jordan Rogove
Cynthia Roubik
Rob Roubik
William Roy
Dina Rozin
Daniel Rubino
John Ruthven
Steve Rybicki
Senthil Sabanayagam
Sal Salahuddin
Martin Salas
Candace Schafer
Sylvia Schnackenburg
Charles Sejud
John Shahlapour
Jochen Silvetti Schmitt
Scott Simmons
Patricia Skermont-
   Pohrte
Mark Spencer
Erich Stenzel
Irina Susorova
Jennifer Sutor
Doug Switzer
Greg Tamborino
Alex Tang
John Thomas
Tracy Trovato

Kara Underwood
John Van Scheltema
Michael Veltman
Allen Villanueva
Anthony Volpe
Heather Weed
Jason Weyland
Clara Wineberg
Roy Witherow
Mark Witte
Pey-Yi Wu
Qi Xu
Ben Yonce
Woong Sun Yoo
James Young

ACKNOWLEDGMENTS AND CREDITS

This book documents what I think of as my mid-course correction—the 20 years after I left Skidmore, Owings & Merrill and the International Style behind and began a series of historical investigations wherein I consciously studied the buildings and styles of earlier eras in an effort to find new sources of architectural inspiration.

I have always loved the beautiful Classical buildings I saw in Paris when I was growing up. In Chicago, I was drawn to the lively architectural eclecticism of the late 19th and early 20th centuries. I gave myself the freedom to be influenced by all of it.

It has been a most rewarding journey. Indeed, I found the inspiration I was looking for. And, ironically, one of the outcomes is that it has led to a renewed interest in Modernism.

I have been aided in this effort by a number of people. First of all, I would like to thank my wife, Jessica, and two sons, Christophe and Remy, for their understanding of and patience with my often impossible schedule.

Building a business while at the same time trying to grow as an artist is harder than I ever imagined it would be. However, I know I could not have accomplished what I have done without their love and support.

I also would like to thank my brother, Michel, who took me in and never stopped encouraging me when I emigrated from France all these many years ago. He was fearless and optimistic, two qualities that continue to define him and which make all the difference when you are starting out.

During the course of this book, I discuss three mentors who influenced me: Peter Collins, Norbert Schoenhauer, and Bruce Graham.

I also would like to acknowledge several other people who either inspired or supported me over the years with their knowledge, advice, and friendship. They are, in no particular order, the late structural genius Fazlur Khan, architect Natalie DeBlois, and builder Harold Schiff.

Is it possible to thank an institution? Why not? Both McGill University in Montreal and Skidmore, Owings & Merrill in Chicago were apt training grounds for a young architect in the 1960s and 70s. They both were places where passion for architecture was actively encouraged.

Finally, I would like to thank my collaborators on this project. This book began with a casual lunch Robert Sharoff and I had two years ago wherein we discussed—as we always do—the state of contemporary architecture and how we could do it all better. Out of that came the notion of a book examining my own efforts in that direction.

After 20 years as an independent architect, my photographic archives were, to put it charitably, a little spotty. We decided to start from scratch using Robert's partner, architectural photographer William Zbaren, to document the work.

The results are deeply satisfying to me. Bill saw the buildings as I do, illuminating not just details and features but also the mood of different projects.

Robert also introduced me to Steve Liska of Liska + Associates, who ultimately became the designer of the book. I had a very specific look in mind for this project. I spend a considerable amount of time in Paris, where a favorite activity is browsing through art books in stores like Le Moniteur and La Hune. I wanted the feel of those books—elegant, quiet, beautiful. Those three adjectives sum up Steve's work.

Lastly, Natalie Phillips joined my office last winter as Communications Manager. Her first assignment was shepherding this book to completion. Her skill, patience, and good humor made it all a lot easier.

Lucien Lagrange

The information and illustrations in this publication have been prepared and supplied by Lucien Lagrange Architects. While all reasonable efforts have been made to source the required information and ensure accuracy, the publishers do not, under any circumstances, accept any responsibility for errors, omissions and representations expressed or implied.